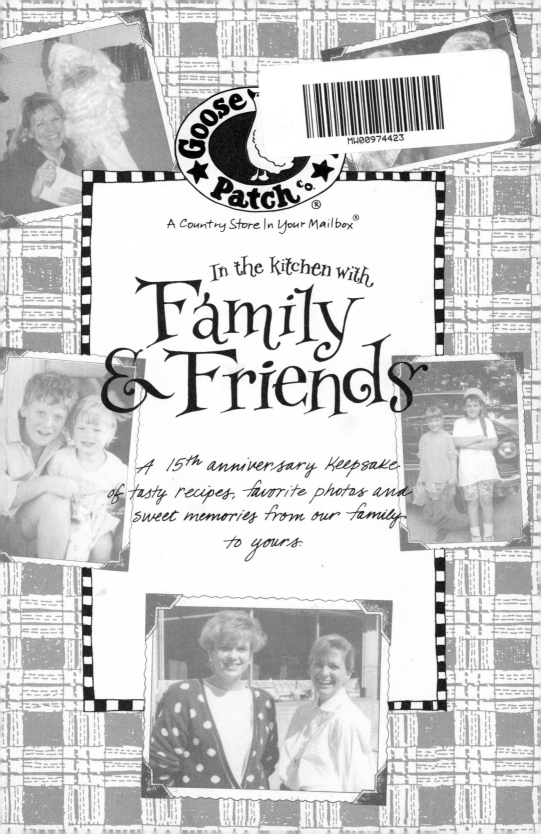

Goose Patch co. ®

A Country Store In Your Mailbox®

In the Kitchen with

Family & Friends

A 15th anniversary Keepsake of tasty recipes, favorite photos and sweet memories from our family to yours.

A Country Store In Your Mailbox®

Gooseberry Patch
149 Johnson Drive
Department BOOK
Delaware, OH 43015
★
1·800·85·GOOSE
1-800·854·6673

Copyright 1999, Gooseberry Patch 1-888-052-32-5
First Printing, April, 1999

How To Subscribe

Would you like to receive
"A Country Store in Your Mailbox"®?
For a 2-year subscription to our 96-page
Gooseberry Patch catalog, simply send $3.00 to:

Gooseberry Patch
149 Johnson Drive
Department BOOK
Delaware, OH 43015

The official Gooseberry Patch "support team!"
Shelby, Emily, Matt, Kyle, Ryan & Jay -1990

Contents

"Remembered joys are never past."
-James Montgomery

Vickie & Jo Ann -1999

Dedication

*To our family and friends, whose encouragement
has been with us each step of the way!*

Appreciation

*A heart-felt "Thanks" to each and every one
of you who helped make our dreams come true!*

Itty Bitty Bites

JoAnn, age 3, with her big brother D.J.

Stuffed Mushrooms

Laura Strausberger
Cary, IL

This recipe came from a dear friend. She brought them to a progressive dinner and they were absolutely wonderful...you can't eat just one!

24 lg. mushrooms
1/2 c. parsley, chopped
1/2 c. green onion, chopped
1/2 c. thyme
3/4 c. butter, divided
16 bacon slices, crisply cooked
    and crumbled

8-oz. pkg. cream cheese,
    softened
2-oz. pkg. fresh Parmesan
    cheese, grated and divided

Rinse and pat dry mushrooms. Remove stems and finely chop. Set caps aside. In medium skillet, sauté mushroom stems, parsley, green onion and thyme with 1/2 cup butter. In large bowl, combine bacon, cream cheese and half the Parmesan cheese. Add sautéed mixture and stir well. Brush mushroom caps with melted butter on both sides. Arrange caps, hollow side up, in oven-proof dish. Fill caps with stuffing and sprinkle the reserved Parmesan cheese on top. Broil 5 to 10 minutes or until heated through the center.

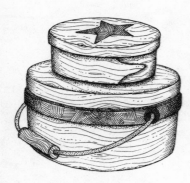

Our very first Gooseberry Patch catalog, mailed in 1985, was sent to just 300 homes. It's hard to believe today so many friends around the world know us as "A Country Store in Your Mailbox®!"

Mini Spinach Pies

Tracey Monnette
Roseville, MI

Whenever I bring these to a get-together, I'm always asked to share the recipe. Many people will tell me they don't like spinach, but will eat 3 or 4 of these! They're quick to make and the results are delicious!

1/4 c. olive oil
1/2 c. onion, chopped
2 eggs, beaten
1 lb. feta cheese, crumbled
3 10-oz. pkgs. frozen chopped
   spinach, thawed and drained

1 t. dried oregano
8-oz. pkg. frozen phyllo dough,
   thawed
2 c. margarine, melted

Preheat oven to 375 degrees. Heat oil in small skillet over medium to high heat. Add onions and cook until transparent. In large bowl, add eggs, onion, feta cheese, spinach and oregano and mix well. Remove phyllo dough from package, unroll and place on large sheet of wax paper. Fold dough crosswise into thirds, using scissors to cut along folds. Cover dough with a clean damp kitchen towel to prevent drying out and cracking. Lay one strip of dough at a time on a flat surface and brush with melted margarine. Fold strip in half lengthwise; brush again. Place rounded teaspoonful of spinach filling on one end of strip; fold one corner to make a triangle. Continue folding end to end as you would a flag, keeping edges straight. Brush top with margarine. Repeat until all filling is used. Place on baking pan or stone, in a single layer, seam side down. Bake 20 minutes or until lightly browned. Serve warm. Makes 5 dozen appetizers.

"Running Gooseberry Patch is a lot of work, but it's difficult to look at it as your 'typical' job because we both have so much fun!"

Vickie
1986

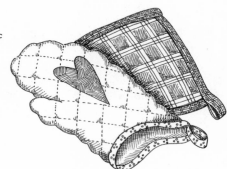

Cheddar Potato Skins

Kathy Grashoff
Ft. Wayne, IN

Potato skins are always a favorite appetizer when our family goes out to eat...now, with this great recipe, we make them at home!

6 med. baking potatoes
1/2 c. Cheddar cheese, finely
   shredded

2 T. green onion, finely chopped
1/8 t. garlic powder
Garnish: salsa and sour cream

Bake potatoes at 425 degrees for 40 to 50 minutes or until tender. Cut each potato lengthwise into quarters. Scoop out insides; leaving 1/2-inch thick shells. Arrange potato shells skin side up on a baking sheet. Spray skins evenly with non-stick coating. Bake uncovered at 425 degrees 20 to 25 minutes or until crisp. Turn potatoes skin side down. Toss together cheese, green onion and garlic powder. Sprinkle cheese mixture over potatoes. Bake about 2 minutes more or until cheese melts. Serve with salsa and sour cream. Makes 24 potato skins.

BLT Dip

Sandy Brinkmeier
Lena, IL

Serve this with an assortment of crackers or sourdough rounds.

2 c. mayonnaise-style salad
   dressing
1 c. sour cream
2 lb. bacon, crisply cooked and
   crumbled

1 med. tomato, chopped
2 green onions, chopped

Combine salad dressing and sour cream until well blended. Add bacon and refrigerate overnight. Fold in remaining ingredients.

Friendship Dip

Sherri Poole
Escondido, CA

Family get-togethers, block parties or any celebration...this easy dip will be an instant family favorite!

1.05 oz. pkg. Italian salad
  dressing mix
2 4-oz. cans chopped green
  chilies
2 5.75 oz. cans olives, chopped

1 bunch green onions, chopped
1 bunch cilantro, chopped
2 to 3 tomatoes, chopped
1 lb. Monterey Jack cheese,
  shredded

Prepare Italian salad dressing mix according to package directions; set aside. Combine remaining ingredients; mix with Italian salad dressing. Refrigerate overnight to allow flavors to blend. Serve with crackers or chips.

Jo Ann & family pose for a portrait -1968

Jalapeño Wraps

Julie Knowles
Escondido, CA

These are fantastic! Even though you use jalapeño peppers, they're not too hot once you remove the seeds.

20 jalapeño peppers, halved
   lengthwise and seeded
8-oz. pkg. cream cheese

1 c. Cheddar cheese, shredded
1/2 lb. bacon slices, halved

Fill each pepper half with cream cheese. Use your fingers to gently press Cheddar cheese into cream cheese filling. Wrap with a piece of bacon and secure with toothpick. Bake at 350 degrees for 20 minutes, or until bacon is done.

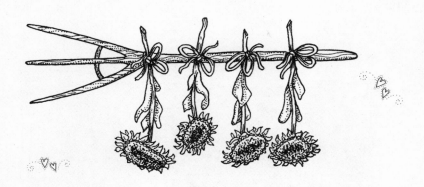

Dear Vickie & Jo Ann,

"When I read your books, it truly feels like I'm entering another world where everyone suddenly becomes my next door neighbor, standing in my kitchen, and sharing with me the secrets of home-cooked meals, the spirit of family traditions and the coziness of what it means to be home again."

Shelly Watts, Indianapolis, IN

Maple Chicken Wings

Donna Nowicki
Center City, MN

The tasty maple and Dijon marinade makes these wings special.

2 to 3 lbs. chicken wings
1 c. maple syrup
2/3 c. chili sauce
1/2 c. onion, finely chopped

2 T. Dijon mustard
2 t. Worcestershire sauce
1/4 to 1/2 t. crushed red pepper
  flakes

Cut chicken wings into 3 sections, discard wing tip section. In a large resealable plastic bag, combine remaining ingredients. Reserve one cup for basting; refrigerate until ready to use. Add chicken to remaining marinade, turning to coat. Seal bag and refrigerate for 4 hours, turning occasionally. Drain and discard marinade. Place chicken in a 13"x9" baking pan. Bake in a 375 degree oven for 30 to 40 minutes basting with the reserved marinade.

"Vickie and I did everything by ourselves in the beginning. We worked from our kitchen tables, basements and extra bedrooms and took turns on phone shifts while watching the kids play in the yard. Some of our very best ideas came while we chatted over the backyard fence!"

Jo Ann
1995

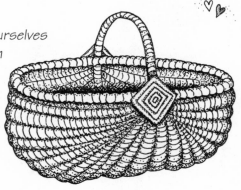

Sharon's Cheese Ball

Sharon Hall
Gooseberry Patch

This is one of our Gooseberry Patch potluck favorites...everyone tells me I make it like no one else. They even think I leave out a "secret" ingredient when I share the recipe!

2 8-oz. pkgs. cream cheese,
   softened
3 T. green onion, chopped
2-1/2 oz. pkg. dried beef, finely
   chopped

2 T. mayonnaise-style salad
   dressing
1 t. Worcestershire sauce
1/2 c. walnuts, chopped

Combine all ingredients well; shape into a ball. Cover cheese ball with walnuts; place in an air tight container. Refrigerate 3 to 4 hours before serving.

"Sharon and my mom were our very first employees. Mother and I have always had a special relationship. Working side by side with her is an experience I will always treasure and one I know she'll never forget!"

Vickie
1990

Bacon-Cheddar Puffs

Betty McKay
Harmony, MN

An easy appetizer with a great combination of flavors! These can be made ahead of time and reheated before you're ready to serve them.

1/2 c. milk
2 T. margarine
1/2 c. all-purpose flour
2 eggs
1/2 c. Cheddar cheese, shredded

4 bacon slices, crisply cooked
   and crumbled
1/4 c. green onion, chopped
1/4 t. garlic salt
1/4 t. pepper

Preheat oven to 350 degrees. Bring milk and margarine to a boil over medium heat. Add flour all at once, stirring until mixture forms a ball. Remove from heat and add eggs one at a time; blend until smooth. Add Cheddar cheese, bacon, green onion, garlic salt and pepper; mix well. Drop by teaspoonfuls on greased cookie sheet. Bake at 350 degrees for 5 to 8 minutes. Makes 3 dozen.

Party Rye Snack Pizzas

Paula Harris
Fruitland Park, FL

These are delicious...enjoy!

1 lb. bulk sausage
1 lb. pasteurized processed
   cheese spread
2 T. catsup

1/8 t. Worcestershire sauce
1/8 t. dried oregano
1/8 t. garlic powder
2 loaves party rye bread

Brown and drain sausage; add remaining ingredients; blend well. Spread on slices of bread. Place bread on an ungreased baking sheet and bake at 450 degrees for 5 minutes or until bubbly.

Green Chili Bites

Glenda Geoghagan
DeFuniak Springs, FL

*When all of my family gets together we love to snack on tempting
appetizers, like these. We serve them at weddings, reunions and
family cookouts. Everyone always asks for the recipe.*

2 4-oz. cans whole green
  chilies, sliced and opened
2 c. Monterey Jack cheese,
  grated

2 c. Cheddar cheese, grated
6 eggs, beaten
salt and pepper to taste

Preheat oven to 325 degrees. Butter an 8" or 9" square baking dish.
Arrange chilies on bottom of baking dish. Mix grated cheeses together
and sprinkle over chilies. Blend eggs, salt and pepper; pour over cheese
and chilies. Bake for 30 to 40 minutes or until firm. Cut into squares
and serve hot. Makes 20 squares.

*"In 1989, we decided to move the business
out of our homes and into a small
storefront in downtown Delaware.
It was a huge step for us then.
But we've always said,
'We're just taking this
day by day.'"*

**Jo Ann
1997**

Jeff's Dried Beef Dip

Sherry Sellers
Sunbury, OH

*Warm slices of French bread or wheat crackers are all
you'll need to serve with this; it's wonderful!*

1/2 c. pecans, chopped
2 T. butter
1/2 t. salt
8-oz. plus 3-oz. pkgs. cream
   cheese, softened
2 T. milk

2-1/2 oz. pkg. dried beef,
   chopped
1/4 c. green pepper, chopped
1 sm. onion, finely chopped
1 c. sour cream
pepper to taste

Combine pecans, butter and salt; spread on a baking sheet. Place in
oven under broiler and lightly toast for 3 to 5 minutes. Remove from
oven and set aside. Mix next 5 ingredients, fold in sour cream and half
the pecan mixture. Place in a 13"x9" baking dish and sprinkle
remaining pecans over top. Bake at 350 degrees for 20 minutes.

"We never dreamed Gooseberry Patch would become
what it is today. We just wanted to try
our hand at something new, but
still be able to spend time at
home with our children. Starting
a country catalog was the
perfect fit."

Vickie
1994

Celebration Deviled Eggs

Barb Bargdill
Gooseberry Patch

Between me, my four brothers and sisters and our children, there are 10 birthdays and 3 anniversaries in the summer months! Along with graduations, Father's Day and the 4th of July, we do a lot of celebrating...any excuse to get together!

12 eggs, hard-boiled
1/2 c. mayonnaise
2 T. onion, chopped
1 t. fresh chives, chopped
1 t. fresh parsley, chopped
1 t. dry mustard

1/2 t. paprika
1/2 t. dried dillweed
1/4 t. salt
1/4 t. pepper
1/4 t. garlic powder
milk

Remove shells from eggs. Cut eggs in half lengthwise and remove yolks. Place yolks in a shallow bowl and mash with a fork. Add rest of ingredients, except milk, to egg yolks. Stir. If necessary, stir in a little milk to achieve the desired consistency. Spoon the yolk mixture into the egg white halves. Cover and chill before serving. Makes 24.

Fresh Veggie Dip

Barbara Obaker
Gibsonia, PA

A good dip for any of your favorite garden vegetables.

1/2 c. mayonnaise
1/2 c. sour cream
1/2 t. seasoned salt flavor
    enhancer

1/2 t. seasoned salt
1/2 t. dillweed
fresh vegetables

Mix all ingredients together; blending well. Serve with a variety of your favorite vegetables.

Salsa-Cheese Twists

Vickie

A great appetizer for graduation parties, potlucks or reunions. If you'd like, you can substitute a milder cheese such as Monterey Jack. Serve them with your favorite dip...ranch, blue cheese or homemade salsa.

1 c. salsa
1/2 c. ranch salad dressing
2 8-oz. tubes crescent rolls

1 c. hot pepper cheese, shredded
fresh cilantro, chopped, to taste

Prepare dip by combing salsa and ranch dressing; mix well. Place in an air-tight container and refrigerate one hour. Lightly oil baking sheets; set aside. Unroll one can of dough into 11"x8" rectangle, press perforations together and sprinkle cheese over dough. Unroll second can of dough; roll into an 11"x8" rectangle, seal perforation marks and lay over cheese. Using a rolling pin, lightly roll dough to press both layers together. Sprinkle desired amount of cilantro over dough, gently pressing into surface of dough. Cut layers of dough into 12 strips, place on lightly oiled baking sheets. Hold down one end of each strip and gently twist 3 or 4 times. Press both ends of twist to baking sheet and bake at 375 degrees for 10 to 15 minutes lightly golden. Serve warm with dip. Serves 12.

Matt, Vickie & Sport...Matt's graduation from high school -1997

Quick Caramel Dip

Terri Vanden Bosch
Rock Valley, IA

One fall day, my mother surprised my children and took them to an apple orchard where they could pick apples together. When they came home, I had this caramel dip ready so we could enjoy their just-picked apples and share the memories made with Grandma.

1 stick butter
14-oz. can sweetened condensed
   milk
14-oz. bag caramels

apple slices
lemon juice
1/2 c. peanuts, optional

Combine first 3 ingredients in a slow cooker for 3 hours; stir occasionally. Serve with fresh slice apples sprinkled with lemon juice to keep them fresh. If desired, peanuts can be folded into the caramel dip before serving. Caramel dip can be refrigerated for one to 2 months.

"We laugh a lot. I think that's the secret to our friendship. Whenever I'm having a bad day, Vickie always knows how to make me laugh and turn that day into a good one."

Jo Ann
1998

Apple-Berry Salsa

*Judy Kelly
St. Charles, MO*

You'll be surprised at how wonderful this is! The cinnamon chips are terrific and it's a nice change from the spicy salsas we're used to.

2 med. Granny Smith apples,
    peeled, cored and chopped
1 c. strawberries, sliced
1 kiwi, peeled and chopped

1 sm. orange
2 T. brown sugar, packed
2 T. apple jelly

Combine apples, strawberries and kiwi; set aside. Zest and juice the orange and add to fruit mixture. Gently blend in remaining ingredients. Serve with cinnamon chips. Makes 2 cups.

Cinnamon Chips:

4 7-inch flour tortillas
1 T. sugar

1/2 t. cinnamon

Lightly spray tortillas with water. Combine sugar and cinnamon and sprinkle over tortillas. Use a pizza cutter to cut each tortilla into 8 wedges; place in a single layer on a baking sheet. Bake 8 to 10 minutes or until lightly browned and crisp. Remove to cooling rack and cool completely.

Dear Vickie & Jo Ann,

"Getting your catalog in today's mail was a treat! I made myself a cup of tea, curled up under an afghan, and spent a delightful afternoon wandering around Gooseberry Patch."

Terry Paulczak
Madison Heights, MI

Waikiki Meatballs

Teresa Beal
Gooseberry Patch

This recipe was shared with me by a dear friend who can always "whip up" a wonderful meal in minutes. The combination of flavors is really good.

1-1/2 lbs. ground beef
2/3 c. cracker crumbs
1/3 c. onion, minced
1 egg
1-1/2 t. salt
1/4 t. ginger
1/4 c. milk

1/2 c. brown sugar, packed
2 T. cornstarch
20-oz. can pineapple tidbits,
   juice reserved
1/3 c. vinegar
1 T. soy sauce
1/4 c. green pepper, chopped

Combine first 7 ingredients; blending well. Shape into one to 2-inch balls and brown in a heavy saucepan; set aside. In a medium saucepan, combine brown sugar and cornstarch; blend in reserved pineapple juice and vinegar. Stir in soy sauce. Add pineapple, green pepper and browned meatballs. Simmer until sauce is warm.

"Sydney is a ray of sunshine. We fell in love with her the second we saw her beautiful smile! She loves looking up to her big brothers and wants to do everything Ryan, Robbie and Kyle do. With four kids and a dog, our home is always filled with giggles and toys...we wouldn't have it any other way!"

Jo Ann
1997

Jo Ann & Sydney at the beach -1997

Itty-Bitty Bites

Creamy Crab Spread

Sara Ercolani
Plains, PA

This recipe is one I turn to for unexpected guests…it's so quick and easy to make! Just serve with crunchy breadsticks.

8-oz. pkg. cream cheese
1 t. milk
1 T. horseradish

1 T. onion, diced
1/2 t. lemon juice
1/2 lb. cooked crab, shredded

Combine all ingredients; blending well. Bake in a one-quart baking dish at 350 degrees for 20 minutes or until top is lightly browned.

5-Layer Taco Dip

Nora Lenahan
Fairless Hills, PA

This will serve quite a few people, but I have found that once my guests try it, I never have enough!

8-oz. pkg. cream cheese,
   softened
1 c. mayonnaise
8 oz. sour cream
12-oz. jar salsa
1 red pepper, chopped

1 green pepper, chopped
16 oz. Monterey Jack cheese,
   shredded
3.8-oz. can sliced black olives,
   optional

Combine cream cheese, mayonnaise and sour cream together. Spread evenly on the bottom of a 13"x9" glass baking dish. Layer in order; salsa, peppers, cheese and black olives. Serve cold.

Spinach Pinwheels

Susan Hurd
Gooseberry Patch

To make rolling the filled tortillas easier, I place each tortilla in the microwave for about 15 seconds before I add the filling.

8-oz. pkg. cream cheese,
   softened
1/2 c. sour cream
1/2 c. mayonnaise
1-oz. pkg. ranch dip mix

3-1/4 oz. jar bacon bits
4 green onions, chopped
2 10-oz. pkgs. frozen chopped
   spinach, thawed and drained
16-oz. pkg. flour tortillas

In a medium mixing bowl, combine cream cheese with sour cream and mayonnaise. Add dry dip mix and combine. Add bacon bits, green onions and spinach; mix well. Spread mix on tortillas to within 1/2 inch of edge and roll up tightly. Wrap each tortilla in plastic wrap and chill overnight. Unwrap and cut each into 1/2-inch slices to serve.

"Gooseberry Patch has always been about sharing. When the first few recipes began arriving in our mailbox I remember thinking, 'This is like exchanging recipes with our neighbors around the country!' That's why we created our cookbooks...it's all about friends sharing with friends!"

Vickie
1992

Burrito Rolls

Connie Wright
Madison, TN

When I make these my daughters line up for the "rejects"...that's what they call the end pieces.

2 8-oz. pkgs. cream cheese, whipped
3 to 4 green onions, sliced
8-oz. pkg. Mexican-blend Cheddar cheese, finely shredded

1-lb. jar mild picante sauce
6-oz. can black olives, drained and chopped
16-oz. pkg. flour tortillas
Garnish: picante sauce

In medium bowl, mix with a blender, cream cheese, green onion, Cheddar cheese and 2 to 3 tablespoons picante sauce. After well blended, stir in black olives. Spread 1-1/2 to 2 tablespoons of cream cheese mixture onto a flour tortilla; roll tortilla tightly. Place on a baking sheet, cover with foil and refrigerate overnight. Slice approximately one inch in width. Place on serving platter with remaining picante sauce in the center.

"When we hired Carolyn, our fourth employee, she worked in the bedroom next to mine. There were evenings where Carolyn would stay for dinner after spending an entire day tapping away on the keyboard upstairs. On Thanksgiving, Carolyn stopped by to try and catch up on some work and she wound up in the kitchen, helping stuff the turkey instead!"

**Jo Ann
1988**

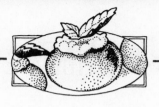

Curry Dip

Kathy Warren
El Dorado, CA

This recipe has been to several potlucks; everyone begs for the recipe!

3 8-oz. pkgs. cream cheese
18-oz. jar apricot preserves
2 T. curry powder

1/2 c. dried cranberries
3/4 c. pistachio nuts, finely
    chopped and divided

Combine cream cheese, preserves and curry with mixer or food processor until well blended. Don't overmix or mixture will be too thin. Stir in 1/2 cup pistachios. Line medium bowl with plastic wrap; spoon mixture into bowl. Refrigerate until ready to use. When ready to serve, turn bowl upside down in middle of a platter and remove bowl. Sprinkle with remaining pistachios and cranberries. Serve with crackers.

Shrimp Salsa

Kathy Staley
Boyd, TX

This is a great hit whenever we serve it.

2-1/2 lbs. cooked shrimp, peeled
    and chopped
24-oz. jar mild salsa
2 c. fresh cilantro, chopped

2 c. tomatoes, chopped
1/2 c. red onion, chopped
2 T. lime juice
tortilla chips

Combine all ingredients in a large bowl. Cover and chill 8 hours or overnight. Serve with tortilla chips.

" 'Gooseberries!' 6-year-old Matt exclaimed when we asked him what we should call our new company. Thirteen years later Matt's graduating from high school and making plans for the future…time sure flies!"

Vickie
1997

Itty-Bitty Bites

Sausage Stars

Geri Peterson
Pleasanton, CA

This is one of my favorite appetizers. To save time, I make the filling ahead and before serving, fill the wrappers and bake!

25-count pkg. won ton wrappers
1 lb. sausage, cooked and
  crumbled
1-1/2 c. sharp Cheddar cheese,
  grated

1-1/2 c. Monterey Jack cheese,
  grated
1 c. ranch-style salad dressing
2-1/4 oz. can sliced black olives
1/2 c. red pepper, chopped

Press one won ton wrapper in each cup of a muffin tin; bake at 350 degrees for 5 minutes. Remove won tons and place on a baking sheet. Repeat with remaining won tons; set aside. Combine remaining ingredients well and fill baked wrappers. Bake at 350 degrees for an additional 5 minutes or until bubbly. Makes 4 to 5 dozen.

"Vickie and I were searching for items to include in our first catalog when we came across the idea for a personalized redware plate. For Christmas that year, I gave Vickie a 'Gooseberry Patch' plate. Imagine my surprise when I opened her gift to me. It was the exact same thing! Who says great minds don't think alike?"

Jo Ann
1985

Veggie Pizza Squares

Donna Dye
London, OH

Try making this traditional favorite with a new twist...puff pastry.

1 sheet puff pastry, thawed
2 t. oil
1 c. broccoli flowerets
1 c. mushrooms, sliced
1/2 c. red pepper, chopped

1 sm. red onion, chopped
3/4 c. spaghetti sauce
1-1/2 c. mozzarella cheese, shredded

Unfold thawed pastry on a lightly floured surface and gently roll into a 15"x10" rectangle. Place on an ungreased baking sheet. Prick pastry with a fork and bake at 400 degrees for 10 minutes. Remove from oven; set aside. Add oil to a medium skillet, cook broccoli, mushrooms, pepper and onion over medium heat until crisp-tender. Spread spaghetti sauce over pastry crust, top with vegetables. Sprinkle cheese over vegetables and bake for an additional 5 minutes or until cheese is bubbly. Let cool slightly then cut into squares.

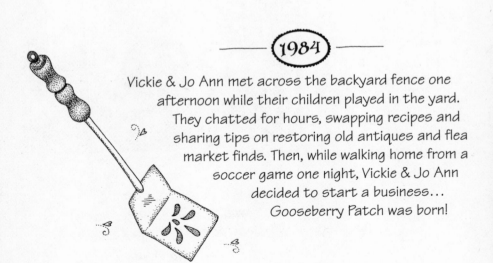

1984

Vickie & Jo Ann met across the backyard fence one afternoon while their children played in the yard. They chatted for hours, swapping recipes and sharing tips on restoring old antiques and flea market finds. Then, while walking home from a soccer game one night, Vickie & Jo Ann decided to start a business...
Gooseberry Patch was born!

Baked Sweet Onion Spread
Valerie Sheppard
Valdosta, GA

Try this spread on crackers, toast points or pita chips. It's a slightly sweet, cheesy spread that's sure to become a new favorite!

1 lg. sweet onion, chopped
1 c. fresh Parmesan cheese,
   grated

1 c. mayonnaise
1/8 t. garlic salt
1/8 t. lemon juice

Mix all ingredients well. Spread in a one-quart baking dish and bake at 350 degrees for 10 minutes or until warm throughout and cheese is melted. Serves 6.

1984

Jo Ann & Vickie originally wanted to open a country store in an old converted schoolhouse, until Vickie's husband, Shelby, suggested they try creating a mail-order catalog.

Parmesan Turkey Strips

Tina Stidam
Delaware, OH

Serve these with a variety of dipping sauces...Dijon mustard,
sweet & sour, barbecue or honey.

8 turkey breasts fillets
1/4 c. milk
1 egg
1/4 t. onion powder
2/3 c. Parmesan cheese, grated

1-1/4 t. dried basil
3/4 t. dried thyme
2/3 c. bread crumbs
1/4 t. pepper

Spray baking sheet with non-stick spray; set aside. Cut turkey into strips. In a small bowl, combine milk and egg; mix well. In a separate bowl, combine remaining ingredients. Dip turkey strips into milk mixture then roll in bread crumb mixture; coating well. Place on baking sheets and bake at 400 degrees for 18 minutes or until golden.

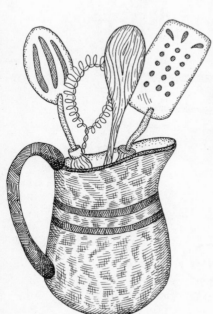

Dear Vickie & Jo Ann,

"When I read your books I can just feel what it's like to grow up with homespun and warm fires; thank you."

Wendy Parker, Portage, MI

Reuben Dip

*Linda Staley
Gooseberry Patch*

I like to serve this with breadsticks, crackers or party rye.

3-oz. pkg. cream cheese
1/4 c. sour cream
1/2 c. Swiss cheese, grated
2 to 3 T. milk

4 oz. sliced corn beef, finely
   diced
1/4 c. chopped sauerkraut,
   drained

Heat all ingredients in a small saucepan over low heat until melted and hot. Thin with additional milk if mixture is too thick.

Hot Party Nuts

*Richard Welsh
Gooseberry Patch*

These nuts have been a family favorite ever since my sister served them at her house-warming. This recipe is delicious with peanuts; even better with cashews!

3/4 lb. nuts
1 egg white
2 t. kosher salt
1 t. sugar

1 t. red pepper flakes
1/2 t. cumin
1/2 t. oregano
1/4 t. cayenne pepper

Toss nuts in egg white; sprinkle seasonings over nuts. Bake at 300 degrees for 25 minutes.

Bacon-Chestnut Appetizers

Carol Christensen
Granby, CT

These yummy appetizers can be made ahead and simply reheated before your guests arrive. I've also substituted chicken or scallops for the chestnuts...wonderful!

1 lb. bacon, sliced in half
2 8-oz. cans whole water
    chestnuts

1/4 c. brown sugar, packed
1/2 c. catsup

Wrap bacon halves around each chestnut and set in an oven proof baking dish. Watching carefully, bake at 325 degrees for 30 minutes. Turn chestnuts and bake an additional 10 minutes. Combine brown sugar and catsup, baste and bake 10 minutes. Toothpicks can be inserted to make serving easier.

Dear Vickie & Jo Ann,

"Your catalog delights my heart. Even the name brings back fond memories of my grandmother's gooseberry pies!"

Ramona Andrews, Long Beach, CA

Southwestern Ranch Dip

*Kristi Hartland
State College, PA*

Prepare this the night before you want to serve it, so all the flavors can blend. Wonderful served with warm tortilla chips!

16 oz. sour cream
3/4 c. mayonnaise
1-oz. pkg. ranch salad dressing
   mix
1-1/4 oz. pkg. taco seasoning
   mix

1/8 t. garlic powder
1/8 t. salt
1/8 t. pepper
4-oz. can chopped green chilies

Combine sour cream and mayonnaise; blending well. Add half of the ranch dressing and half of the taco seasoning; mix well. Reserve remaining halves for another use. Stir in garlic powder, salt, pepper and green chilies. Place in a covered container and refrigerate at least 2 hours or overnight.

Dear Vickie & Jo Ann,

"I have been a customer of your company almost from the beginning. I receive many catalogs through the mail, but none even come close to yours. Keep up the good work...you are appreciated more than you know!"

Sherry Barnhart, Portland, OR

Ryan as Abe Lincoln in
a school play - 1989

Jo Ann & Vickie:...first day in
our new building! - 1997

Kaiser with his buddies
Robbie & Kyle - 1996

Ryan with Grandpa &
Grandma Martin - 1984

Sunday-Best Soups

JoAnn, 2 ½, with her sister Gail and brother D.J.

Spicy Soup

Amy Lawson
Topeka, KS

We love this served with flour tortillas or homemade cornbread. It doesn't take all day to prepare, but it tastes as if it did.

1 lb. ground beef, browned
10-1/2 oz. can beef broth
14-1/2 oz. can tomatoes
4-oz. can green chilies
15-1/2 oz. can kidney beans
15-1/4 oz. can corn

15-oz. can tomato sauce
1 bunch green onions, chopped
1 T. cumin
fresh cilantro to taste
salt and pepper to taste

Combine all ingredients in a large stockpot; bring to a low boil. Simmer over medium heat for 30 minutes.

Chicken Stew

Joanne West
Beavercreek, OH

Let the slow cooker do all the work for you!

2 lg. sweet potatoes, peeled and
   chopped
1 med. onion, sliced
6 boneless chicken breasts
1/2 t. dried thyme

1/4 t. pepper
2 bay leaves
3-1/2 c. water, divided
2 2.8 oz. pkgs. chicken flavor
   ramen noodle soup

In a 3-quart slow cooker, layer potatoes, onion and chicken. Sprinkle with thyme and pepper. Add bay leaves. Combine one cup water and seasoning packets from noodle soup; reserve noodles, pour over chicken. Add remaining water to stockpot. Cover, cook over low heat 7 hours. Stir in reserved noodles, turn heat to high and cook 10 minutes.

Crab Bisque

Judy Kelly
St. Charles, MO

You'll love this rich, creamy soup...it makes a wonderful meal.

6 T. butter, divided
4 T. green pepper, finely chopped
4 T. onion, finely chopped
1 green onion, finely chopped
2 T. parsley, finely chopped
2 T. all-purpose flour

1 c. milk
1/8 t. salt
1 t. pepper
1-1/2 c. half-and-half
1 c. crab meat

Heat 4 tablespoons butter in skillet. Add green pepper, onion, green onion and parsley. Sauté 5 minutes. In saucepan, over low heat, combine remaining butter and flour. Stir until blended. Add milk and blend over medium heat until thickened. Stir in salt and pepper; add sautéed vegetables. Blend in half-and-half. Bring to a boil; reduce heat and add crab. Simmer uncovered 5 minutes. Makes 4 servings.

"We had very little business experience between us when we started Gooseberry Patch. Jo Ann set up the computer and kept track of the finances; I was busy designing new catalogs and keeping in touch with all of our friends from across the country. Everything we've learned about running the business is 'self-taught.'"

**Vickie
1995**

Mom's Tender Beef Stew

Kara Allison
Gooseberry Patch

I used to love coming home from school to see a big pot of beef stew on the stove and popovers in the oven. I remember it being so yummy and it especially hit the spot after a cold field hockey game in late autumn.

2 lbs. boneless beef chuck,
    cubed
1 clove garlic, minced
1 med. onion, sliced
6 carrots, quartered
8 sm. whole onions
3 med. potatoes, peeled and
    cubed
1 t. lemon juice
1 t. Worcestershire sauce

1 bay leaf
2 t. salt
1/4 t. pepper
4 c. water
1/8 t. allspice
1 t. sugar
1/2 c. all-purpose flour
1 t. browning sauce
1/2 c. cold water

Combine all ingredients, except last 3, in a Dutch oven. Cover and bake at 350 degrees for 4 hours or until meat is tender. Remove from oven; set aside. In a jar with a tight fitting lid, mix remaining 3 ingredients; shake until well blended. Stir into stew, boil one minute, remove from heat. Serves 5.

Shelby, Vickie & Emily snuggle up for a cozy Christmas photo -1987

Meatball & Escarole Soup
Maureen Sanchirico
Cherry Hill, NJ

I've been enjoying this soup during the cold winter months for as long as I can remember. As children, my sisters and I would come home after playing in the cold snow to a house filled with the aroma of this soup.

1 lb. ground beef	1 T. olive oil
1/2 c. bread crumbs	2 green onions, thinly sliced
1/4 c. grated Parmesan cheese	2 14-1/2 oz. cans beef broth
1/4 t. salt	1/2 t. dried marjoram
1/4 t. pepper	1 sm. bunch escarole, torn
1 lg. egg	1 lg. tomato, cubed
3-1/4 c. water, divided	

In large bowl, combine beef, bread crumbs, Parmesan cheese, salt, pepper, egg and 1/4 cup water. Shape mixture into 30 meatballs. Add olive oil to a 5-quart Dutch oven over medium-high heat. Brown half the meatballs, set aside and repeat with remaining meatballs. Cook green onions for one minute in the drippings remaining in the Dutch oven. Add broth, marjoram, meatballs and 3 cups of water. Over high heat, bring to a boil. Immediately reduce heat to low, cover and simmer 5 minutes. Stir in escarole and tomato; heat thoroughly. Serves 6.

"We started Gooseberry Patch because we found that many of the antiques we enjoyed had become so expensive. We wanted to give people the look of country antiques at reasonable prices."

Jo Ann
1989

Creamy Chicken Soup

Carol Koluncich
Santa Barbara, CA

A friend from the school PTA shared this recipe with me. Not only does our family love it, it's always a hit when I take it to church suppers.

1 t. salt
1/2 t. pepper
1 qt. plus 1 c. chicken broth,
 divided
4-oz. med. egg noodles
1/2 c. butter, melted

3/4 c. onion, chopped
3/4 c. celery, chopped
3/4 c. carrot, chopped
2 T. all-purpose flour
1 qt. milk, warmed

Add salt and pepper to chicken broth. Bring one quart chicken broth to a boil and add noodles, cooking until tender. Combine butter, one cup broth and vegetables, cook until vegetables are tender. Add flour into vegetable mixture and stir until smooth. Cook for 5 minutes over low heat. Add flour mixture to noodles and broth and cook until thick. Add milk and simmer 5 minutes. Remove from heat, season to taste. Makes 6 to 8 servings.

The first Gooseberry Patch cookbook, "Old-Fashioned Country Christmas," was inspired by hundreds of letters, recipes, tips, family memories and photos received from our country friends around the country.

Potato-Mushroom Chowder

*Julie Ho
Minneapolis, MN*

We really enjoy this hearty soup during our chilly Minnesota winters.

1/2 lb. fresh mushrooms,
   coarsely chopped
1 med. onion, chopped
2 T. butter, melted
1-1/2 c. potatoes, diced
1 c. boiling water
2 c. milk
2 egg yolks, beaten

1/4 c. sherry or dry white wine
2 c. sour cream
1/4 t. thyme leaves
1/8 t. cloves
1/8 t. mace
1/8 t. salt
1/8 t. white pepper
Garnish: parsley, chopped

Sauté mushrooms and onion in butter for about 4 minutes. Add potatoes and boiling water. Bring mixture to a boil; cover. Cook 10 minutes or until potatoes are tender; do not drain water. Blend in milk. Mix egg yolks with sherry or white wine and sour cream; stir into soup. Heat thoroughly, but do not bring to a boil. Add cloves, mace, salt and pepper. Sprinkle with parsley.

1999

Vickie loves to work on craft projects. One of her favorites includes decorating old hat boxes with family photos to create "memory boxes" for her children Matt and Emily.

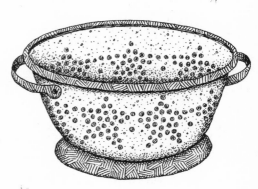

Red Pepper Soup

Donna Nowicki
Center City, MN

Spicy, but not too hot, it's a nice change from traditional rice soups.

6 med. red peppers, chopped
2 med. carrots, chopped
2 med. onions, chopped
1 celery stalk, chopped
4 cloves garlic, minced
1 T. olive oil
64-oz. can of chicken broth
1/2 c. long grain rice, uncooked

2 t. dried thyme
1-1/2 t. salt
1/4 t. pepper
1/8 to 1/4 t. cayenne pepper
1/8 to 1/4 t. crushed red pepper
    flakes

In large Dutch oven, sauté red peppers, carrots, onions, celery and garlic in olive oil until tender. Stir in the broth, rice, thyme, salt, pepper and cayenne pepper; bring to a boil. Reduce heat; cover and simmer for 20 to 25 minutes or until the vegetables and rice are tender. Cool for 30 minutes. Purée in small batches, return to pan and add red pepper flakes. Heat through.

Cowboy Stew

Crystal Lappie
Worthington, OH

This easy recipe can also be made in a slow cooker.

3 lbs. stew beef
1-1/2 oz. pkg. dry onion soup

10-3/4 oz. can mushroom soup

Place beef in an oven-proof dish. Sprinkle soup mix over beef; spoon mushroom soup on top. Fill empty soup can with water, add to dish. Cover and bake at 350 degrees for 3 hours. Serves 6 to 8.

Taco Soup

Sharon Andrews
Gooseberry Patch Artisan

As a busy doll designer I am always looking for something quick and easy to prepare for dinner. This recipe was given to me by one of my dearest friends, thank you Melinda, and is a big hit around the Andrews' house.

1 lb. ground beef
1 med. onion, chopped
14.5-oz. can diced tomatoes
14.5-oz. can tomatoes and
   green chilies
15-1/4 oz. can corn, undrained
15-1/4 oz. can hominy,
   undrained
15.8-oz. can Great Northern
   beans, undrained

16-oz. can pinto beans,
   undrained
14-1/2 oz. can chicken broth
1-1/4 oz. pkg. taco seasoning
1-oz. pkg. dry Ranch dressing
Garnish: Cheddar cheese, grated
   and tortilla chips

Combine all ingredients in a large stockpot. Bring to a simmer and cook 30 minutes. Spoon into individual serving bowls and top with Cheddar cheese and tortilla chips.

Happy Birthday Sydney! -1998

"*Sydney and her grandma share the same birthday...September 29th! Sydney was quite the comedian at the party, modeling her new sombrero for all to see. Even the waitress couldn't stop laughing!*"

Jo Ann
1998

Cream of Broccoli Soup

Cindy Cornelissen
Milton Mills, NH

This soup is always a hit whenever I serve it, so be prepared...you'll be asked to share the recipe!

1-1/2 c. fresh broccoli, chopped
6 chicken bouillon cubes
1/4 c. onion, finely chopped
1 t. thyme
1/8 t. garlic powder
1/2 t. salt

2 c. water
1/2 c. butter
1 c. all-purpose flour
2 c. milk
1/4 t. pepper

Combine broccoli, bouillon cubes, onion, thyme, garlic powder, salt and water; bring to a boil. Simmer for 15 minutes. Don't drain. Melt butter in a saucepan, remove from heat and stir in flour; blend well. Add milk and pepper. Stir in broccoli mixture. Cook over medium heat stirring constantly until soup thickens.

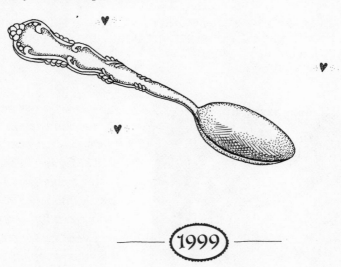

1999

Gooseberry Patch today is still very much the same as it was in 1984...two country friends having fun!

White Chili

Kathy Williamson
Delaware, OH

*A new version of the traditional chili recipe; you'll be
surprised how much you'll like it!*

1 lb. Great Northern beans
4 c. chicken broth
1 clove garlic, minced
1 sm. onion, chopped
4-oz. can green chilies, chopped

1-1/2 t. chili powder
4 c. chicken, cooked and
    chopped
Garnish: 3 c. Monterey Jack
    cheese, shredded

Place beans in a Dutch oven, cover with water and soak overnight;
drain. Combine beans, broth, garlic and onion. Bring mixture to a boil.
Reduce heat and simmer 3 hours. Add chili powder and chicken,
simmer one hour longer. Spoon into bowls and garnish with cheese.
Serves 8 to 10.

Dear Vickie & Jo Ann,

"Gooseberry Patch is truly country from the heart! My little
kitchen makes me feel all warm and merry because it's done in
all Gooseberry!"

Florine Hase, Mesa, AZ

New England Chowder

Jan Walsh
Gooseberry Patch Artisan

When we have fresh clams, called steamers here in the northeast,
I use this recipe to make clam chowder...a delicious meal.

3 slices bacon
1 to 2 lg. onions, chopped
4 lg. potatoes, peeled and
   chopped
20 clams, steamed and chopped

4 to 6 c. water or clam broth
1 t. fresh thyme
1 bay leaf
1 t. fresh parsley
1 pt. cream

In a large skillet, sauté bacon and onions over low heat, until onions are transparent. Remove bacon; set aside. Place potatoes in a stockpot cover with water and boil until just tender; drain. Combine potatoes, clams, water or clam broth and herbs to skillet. Over low heat, cook until heated through. In a separate saucepan, warm cream over low heat; blend into soup mixture. Remove bay leaf before serving.

Chicken Noodle Soup

Ruth Hurst
West Memphis, AR

My family looks forward to this soup as soon as the weather's cool.

6 chicken breasts, cooked and
   shredded, broth reserved
12-oz. pkg. wide noodles
1 med. onion, chopped

4-oz. can sliced mushrooms
2 t. butter
1 pt. half-and-half
24 slices American cheese

Cook noodles in chicken broth, according to package directions. Sauté onion and mushrooms in butter, add to noodles; stir in chicken. Blend in half-and-half and cheese. Simmer 30 minutes over low heat.

Cheesy Vegetable Soup

Ramona Andrews
Long Beach, CA

This is my favorite recipe...I always get compliments and hugs when I serve it. In our family, we can never have too much of this wonderful soup!

1 c. carrots, finely chopped
3/4 c. celery, finely chopped
3/4 c. onion, finely chopped
1/2 c. butter
1 c. biscuit baking mix
1/2 t. paprika
1/2 t. pepper

1/2 t. cayenne pepper
14-1/2 oz. chicken broth
2 c. half-and-half
2 c. sharp Cheddar cheese, grated
6 potatoes, boiled and diced

Cook carrots, celery and onion in butter in a 4-quart Dutch oven until celery and onion are transparent. Stir in biscuit baking mix, paprika, pepper and cayenne pepper; remove from heat. Gradually, stir in chicken broth. Heat to boiling over medium heat, stirring constantly. Boil and stir one minute. Reduce heat, stir in half-and-half, cheese and potatoes. Heat until cheese is melted. Makes 6 to 8 servings.

Bet you can't get this Gooseberry gang to say "Cheese"!
Matt, Max, Emily, Kyle & Ryan -1988

Chicken-Tortellini Soup

Laura Fitch
Hampton, VA

This is great for a fall picnic. Fill a container with soup, bring a loaf of warm homemade bread and you have a great meal!

4 to 6 chicken breasts, cooked
   and boned, broth reserved
3 10-1/2 oz. cans chicken broth
1 clove garlic, minced
1-1/2 c. carrots, sliced
1 med. onion, chopped
2 10-3/4 oz. cans cream of
   chicken soup

16-oz. pkg. frozen chopped
   broccoli
9-oz. pkg. fresh spinach or
   cheese tortellini
1/2 t. pepper
1 t. basil

In a large stockpot combine reserved chicken broth, canned chicken broth and garlic. Add carrots and onion to stockpot and cook until tender. Add chicken and cream of chicken soup; stir well. Stir in broccoli, tortellini, pepper and basil. Simmer 15 minutes, or until the broccoli is just light green and tortellini is tender.

1999

All of our Gooseberry Patch catalogs
are designed with warm friendships
and plenty of smiles in mind!
Our Gooseberry circle of
friends grows with each
new catalog we mail!

Sunday-Best Soups

Vegetable Soup with Beef

Sarah Goggans
Olathe, KS

I've never had leftovers of this easy delicious soup. Quick to make, it's a hearty family dinner at the end of a busy day.

1 lb. lean ground beef, browned
   and drained
14-1/2 oz. can stewed tomatoes
15-1/2 oz. can tomato sauce
1-1/2 oz. pkg. dry onion soup
   mix

10-1/2 oz. can beef broth
15-oz. pkg. frozen mixed
   vegetables

Mix all above ingredients together in a slow cooker. Stir in one soup can of water. Cook on low temperature 8 to 12 hours.

"Remember Sunday dinner at Grandma's house and her favorite recipe for buttery mashed potatoes? We've received so many wonderful recipes from around the country through the years. There's something very special about having a treasured recipe selected for one of our books and seeing your name in print!"

Vickie
1998

Spicy Garden Chili

Jo Ann

Mexican-style seasonings and two types of beans make this chili special. We like it served with jalapeño cornbread!

1 T. vegetable oil
1 c. onions, chopped
1 c. celery, sliced
1 t. garlic, finely chopped
1 c. vegetable broth
28-oz. can tomatoes, chopped
15-oz. can red beans, rinsed and drained
15-1/2 oz. can lima beans, rinsed and drained

1 T. chili powder
2 T. fresh basil leaves, chopped
1 t. sugar
1/2 t. cumin
1/4 t. red pepper
Garnish: sour cream and fresh cilantro, chopped

In 3-quart saucepan heat oil; add onions, celery and garlic. Cook over medium-high heat, stirring occasionally, for 3 to 4 minutes or until tender. Stir in all remaining ingredients. Continue cooking until mixture comes to a full boil. Reduce heat to low and cover saucepan. Continue to cook, stirring occasionally for 15 minutes. Top each serving with sour cream and cilantro.

Dear Vickie & Jo Ann,

"Since I live in Australia, I really love looking through your catalog and books at all the wonderful things that I am unable to find here. All of my friends here love the recipes and decorating tips in your books! Unfortunately, it does make me homesick sometimes! But I love looking at the books over a cup of tea! Thanks so much for all of your wonderful ideas!"

Anita Grant, Victoria, Australia

Dad's Sausage Soup

Carol Burns
Gooseberry Patch

On cold and rainy football Saturdays, Dad's soup warms our family and friends during halftime. He always stops by the baker's for a delicious loaf or two of warm bread to serve alongside it.

4 oz. hot Italian sausage links, thickly sliced
4 oz. sweet Italian sausage links, thickly sliced
1/2 c. onions, chopped
2 lg. potatoes, peeled and sliced

2 14-1/2 oz. cans chicken broth
10-oz. pkg. frozen chopped spinach
1/2 c. water
1/4 t. pepper

In a large saucepan brown the sausages and onion until tender. Drain fat. Add potatoes, chicken broth, spinach, water and pepper. Bring to a boil; reduce heat. Cover and simmer about 20 minutes or until potatoes are tender. Makes 6 servings.

Kyle, Jay & Ryan take a break from decorating the family Christmas tree to smile for the camera -1992

Hearty Corn Chowder

Martine Fusco
South Glastonbury, CT

My family holds a reunion every August, and we always enjoy fresh corn. One year when we had unusually cold weather, we made this chowder. It was such a hit that we've continued making it every year!

1 c. celery, chopped
1/2 c. onion, chopped
1/2 lb. bacon, crisply cooked
   and crumbled, drippings
   reserved
2 c. potatoes, peeled and diced
1 c. water

2 c. fresh corn
14-3/4 oz. can cream-style corn
12-oz. can evaporated milk
6 oz. smoked sausage links,
   sliced
1 t. dillweed

Sauté celery and onion in 2 tablespoons bacon drippings until lightly browned. Add potatoes and water. Cover and cook over medium heat for 10 minutes. Stir in fresh and cream-style corn, milk, sausage, dill and crumbled bacon. Cook until the potatoes are tender, about 30 to 40 minutes. Makes 4 to 6 servings.

More than 2 million copies of Gooseberry Patch cookbooks have been printed since 1992!

Tomato-Basil Soup

Denise Rounds
Tulsa, OK

Fresh basil makes this creamy soup so tasty.

8 to 10 tomatoes, peeled, cored
   and chopped
4 c. tomato juice
12 to 14 fresh basil leaves
1 c. heavy cream

2 T. sweet, unsalted butter
salt to taste
1/4 t. black pepper
Garnish: fresh basil leaves

Combine tomatoes and tomato juice in a saucepan; simmer 30 minutes. Remove from heat and purée, a little at a time, with basil leaves. Return to saucepan. Stirring constantly over low heat, add cream, butter, salt and pepper. Garnish with basil leaves.

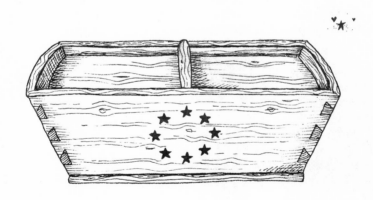

Dear Vickie & Jo Ann,

"No matter if you live in a city or the suburbs, you always feel at home with Vickie & Jo Ann at Gooseberry Patch!"

Stacey Pineda, Foster City, CA

Family Favorite Bean Soup

Barbara Bargdill
Gooseberry Patch

This is our favorite bean soup because it's so hearty and easy to make. It's great to serve in big mugs so the kids can carry them into the family room for a casual meal.

2 c. mixed dry beans
3 qts. water
1 ham hock
1 t. salt
3 chicken bouillon cubes
2 cloves garlic, minced
2 c. celery, chopped

1-1/2 c. onion, chopped
14-1/2 oz. can tomatoes
1 T. dried parsley
1 t. dried basil
1 bay leaf
1/4 t. dried thyme
2 c. carrots, diced

Wash and drain the beans. Place beans in a large stockpot, add water, ham hock, salt and bouillon cubes. Cover and simmer for 2-1/2 to 3 hours. Add remaining ingredients and simmer for 1-1/2 to 2-1/2 hours longer. Remove bay leaf and serve.

"Every year we take a special trip as a family at Christmastime. The boys have a ball at the beach with their little sister Sydney! Some of my most treasured memories are of family vacations...this trip will always be special to me!"

Jo Ann
1998

Family vacation... Sydney, Ryan, Robbie, Kyle & Jo Ann -1998

Sunday-Best Soups

Herbed Celery Soup

Kathy Wyatt
Concord, CA

A soup that's a terrific change of pace. The toasted French bread and sprinkle of nutmeg really are wonderful!

4 T. butter, melted
4 c. celery, finely chopped
2 t. dried chives
1-1/2 t. dried tarragon
1/2 t. dried chervil

8 c. chicken broth
1/4 t. sugar
salt and pepper to taste
8 slices French bread, toasted
Garnish: nutmeg

In a medium saucepan, add butter, celery, chives, tarragon and chervil. Cover and cook for 5 minutes or until celery has softened. Add the chicken broth, sugar, salt and pepper; simmer over low heat for 20 minutes. Just before serving, toast the bread and place a slice in each serving bowl, then ladle in soup. Garnish with a pinch of nutmeg.

Libby's Oyster Chowder

Juanita Williams
Jacksonville, OR

One of 10 children, Aunt Libby was born at the end of World War II. In celebration of the end of the war she was named Liberty Belle; this soup is one of her specialities.

1 doz. oysters, liquid reserved
4 T. onion, chopped
2 T. shortening
3 c. potatoes, cooked and cubed

1-1/2 t. salt
1/8 t. pepper
4 c. milk, scalded
2 T. all-purpose flour

Chop oysters and add to a saucepan with onions and shortening. Cook until onions are lightly browned. Add potatoes, salt, pepper and milk; bring to a boil. Combine flour and enough water to form a paste; blend into chowder. Add reserved oyster liquid. Stir until chowder thickens.

Mushroom-Seafood Chowder   *Vickie*

So yummy on a chilly autumn day!

2 slices bacon, crisply cooked
   and crumbled, drippings
   reserved
3 c. mushrooms, sliced
3 leeks, white parts only, sliced
2 cloves garlic, minced
3 med. potatoes, chopped
2 14-1/2 oz. cans chicken broth
1/4 t. pepper

1 lg. carrot, shredded
3 T. margarine, melted
3 T. all-purpose flour
2 c. half-and-half
8 oz. fresh shrimp, peeled
8 oz. fresh scallops

In a large skillet, combine reserved bacon drippings with mushrooms, leeks and garlic. Cook over medium heat until mushrooms and leeks are tender. Add potatoes, broth and pepper to skillet; bring to a boil. Reduce heat to low and cook, covered, until potatoes are tender. Add shredded carrot to skillet and bring to a boil. Blend together margarine and flour, add alternately to chowder with half-and-half, Bring to a simmer; add shrimp, scallops and bacon. Continue to cook until shrimp are pink, 4 to 5 minutes. Serves 10 to 12.

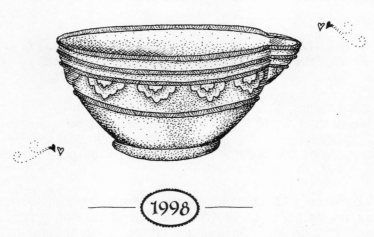

1998

The very first full-color Gooseberry Patch catalog was the
Spring 1998 issue!

Slow Cooker Goulash

Wendy Paffenroth
Pine Island, NY

This family favorite was not originally created for the slow cooker, but when it became popular and my mother went back to work, she adapted her recipe to the new "gadget."

2 lbs. stew beef
1/4 c. oil
2 28-oz. cans potatoes, drained
   and rinsed
4 carrots, peeled and sliced
1 t. marjoram
8-oz. can tomato sauce

3 c. water
1 clove garlic, minced
1/2 t. salt
1 t. lemon zest
2 beef bouillon cubes
1 T. paprika

Brown beef with oil in a medium skillet; set aside. In a 5-quart slow cooker, combine potatoes, carrots, meat and remaining ingredients. Cover and cook on high for 4 hours or on low for 7 hours. Makes 4 to 5 servings.

"Some of the best recipes I've ever served started in the kitchens of friends. As a teacher, I always had an opportunity to swap a recipe or two. My collection grew from there. Soon I was filling kitchen drawers, pantry shelves, shoe boxes and just about anything I could find with recipe cards. Maybe someday I'll get around to organizing them!"

Jo Ann
1991

friends are flowers in the garden of life

Carrot-Parsnip Soup

Donna Winarski
Tucson, AZ

My favorite soup because it's easy to prepare, and it reminds my family of cozy winter afternoons.

2 T. butter
2 lg. slices sweet onion, diced
1 sm. parsnip, peeled and sliced
1 lb. carrots, peeled and sliced
1 med. russet potato, diced

2 14-1/2 oz. cans chicken broth
1/8 t. garlic powder
pepper to taste
1/4 c. half-and-half
Garnish: croutons

Melt butter in a large saucepan; sauté onion 2 minutes. Add parsnip, carrots and potato; sauté 8 minutes. Add enough water to the chicken broth to equal 4 cups and blend into saucepan with garlic powder and pepper. Cover saucepan, reduce heat and simmer for 45 minutes. Purée mixture in blender; return to saucepan and heat. Slowly blend in half-and-half, stirring constantly. Heat through but not to boiling. Top with croutons. Serves 4.

"My most favorite memories of staying at Grandma's house were the smell of fresh cinnamon rolls on Saturday morning, the gentle sound of rain on the tin roof where we slept, the smell of the wood stove she cooked on and the water we pumped from the well."

Vickie
1999

Sausage-Cheese Soup

Linda Staley
Gooseberry Patch

I usually make this soup on cold, rainy days. It's so hearty, it warms our family right up!

1/4 c. margarine, melted
2 carrots, shredded
1 celery stalk, thinly sliced
1/4 c. all-purpose flour
1/8 t. pepper

4 c. milk
8 oz. smoked sausage, sliced
2 c. American or Swiss cheese, shredded

In a large saucepan, combine margarine, carrots and celery; cook until tender. Stir in flour and pepper until well blended. Add milk and sausage. Stirring constantly, cook over medium heat 8 minutes or until mixture is thick and bubbly. Cook for one minute more. Blend in cheese and continue to stir until cheese is melted. Makes 4 servings.

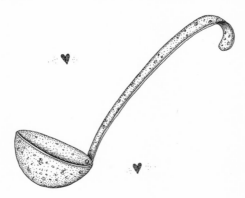

Dear Vickie & Jo Ann,

"My grandmother had a small gooseberry patch that I spent summer evenings in tasting the tart green berries or watching them turn pink and anticipating a mouthful of tangy gooseberry jelly. This is one 'smile' your catalog brings to mind."

Sandy Woodyard, Narrows, VA

Beef & Barley Soup

Sandy Benham
Sanborn, NY

When winter's on its way, here's a pot of soup we always prepare.

1-1/2 lbs. stew beef, cubed
2 c. potatoes, chopped
1 c. celery, sliced
1-1/2 c. dried barley, cooked and
    strained

1 T. celery salt
2 T. pepper
1 c. mushrooms, sliced

Place meat in saucepan with 3 inches of water. Simmer one hour or until tender. Remove beef; reserving broth. In a separate saucepan, combine potatoes and celery; cover with water and cook until tender. Add beef, broth and barley. Simmer on low for 30 minutes. Add seasonings and mushrooms. Simmer for 15 minutes.

Pumpkin Soup

Dorothy Foor
Jeromesville, OH

For an easier version I substitute frozen, cooked squash.

1/2 c. cashews, chopped
1 sm. cooking pumpkin

1 T. fresh ginger, grated
salt to taste

Soak cashews in water for several hours. Cut pumpkin in half and remove seeds. Bake at 350 degrees, cut side down, for 45 minutes to one hour. Remove pumpkin from peel and purée. Add to a stock pot. Purée cashews until smooth and add to pumpkin. Add enough water until soup is desired thickness. Add ginger and salt, heat through.

Indian Summer Soup

Sammy Polizzi-Morrison
Aurora, CO

Growing up, my family always made this soup in the autumn and we'd take a big bowl outside to enjoy by the family bonfire.

1 med. onion, chopped
1/4 c. olive oil
1-1/2 lbs. ground beef
2 15-1/4 oz. cans corn
15-1/2 oz. can black beans
16-oz. can pinto beans
15-1/2 oz. can red beans

15-1/2 oz. can kidney beans
14-1/2 oz. can stewed tomatoes
1 to 2 tomatoes, chopped
fresh garlic to taste
1 to 2 T. taco seasoning
1 carrot, sliced

Cook onion in olive oil until tender, add beef and brown; drain oil. Add remaining ingredients and simmer 30 to 45 minutes.

Vickie at a country inn -1992

"On a visit to New England in 1992, we came across this giant Jack-o'-Lantern on the front lawn of a country restaurant. I just couldn't resist and we snapped this quick photo!"

Vickie
1992

Italian Sausage Stew

Linda McClain
Columbia, NJ

I think this stew tastes even better reheated to enjoy the next day.

1 lb. Italian sausage, thickly
   sliced
1 T. olive or vegetable oil
1 c. onion, diced
1 clove garlic, minced
1 c. carrots, sliced
1 t. dried basil
2 sm. zucchini, diced
1-lb. can chopped tomatoes,
   undrained

10-oz. can beef broth
2 c. cabbage, finely shredded
1 t. salt
1/4 t. pepper
15.8-oz. can Great Northern
   beans, undrained
1 c. small pasta

In a deep saucepan, brown sausage in oil. Add onion, garlic, carrots and basil; cook 5 minutes. Stir in zucchini, tomatoes, beef broth, cabbage, salt and pepper. Bring stew to a boil; reduce heat and simmer, covered, for one hour. Add beans and cook an additional 10 minutes. Stir in pasta and cook 10 minutes. Makes 8 servings.

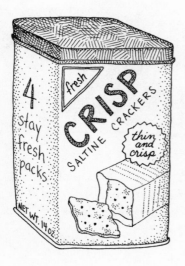

1999

Gooseberry Patch mails millions of catalogs around the world annually. We've received orders from as far away as Iceland, Germany, Australia, Japan, Great Britain, Italy, France and New Zealand!

Soup Georgette

Robbin Chamberlain
Gooseberry Patch

I grew up on a large farm where my mother always tended a garden. When she prepared this soup, everything except the celery came straight out of the garden; still warm from the sun. You can imagine how fresh and delicious it was! She always served this with her own special recipe for southern cornbread.

5 or 6 tomatoes, peeled,
   quartered and seeded
1 sm. bunch celery, thinly sliced
2 leeks, thinly sliced
3 to 4 lbs. carrots, thinly sliced
2 T. butter
1 T. all-purpose flour

2-1/2 c. water
1/8 t. sugar
1/2 bay leaf
1/8 t. nutmeg
5 T. light cream
Garnish: 1 T. fresh parsley

Place tomatoes through a sieve, reserving juice and tomatoes. Sauté celery, leeks and carrots in butter until soft, but not brown. Stir in flour, reserved tomatoes and tomato juice, 2-1/2 cups water, sugar, bay leaf and nutmeg. Stir over medium heat until mixture comes to a boil. Reduce heat, add cream and simmer soup 30 minutes. Remove bay leaf; discard. Purée soup in a blender. Garnish with parsley.

"In just six short years, our Gooseberry Patch catalog has doubled in size! Who knows where we'll be 10 years from now?"

Jo Ann
1990

Fireside Potato Chowder

Carol Bull
Delaware, OH

*A thick chowder that's just right to take the chill out of a family day
spent building snowmen or having a snowball fight!*

3 c. potatoes, chopped
1 c. water
2/3 c. onion, finely chopped
1 t. dried marjoram, crushed
1/2 t. dry mustard
2 t. instant chicken bouillon

1/4 t. pepper
3 c. milk, divided
1/4 c. all-purpose flour
3/4 c. Swiss cheese, shredded
1 c. ham, chopped
2 T. fresh parsley, chopped

Add potatoes to a large stockpot, cover with water. Add onion,
marjoram, mustard, bouillon and pepper. Bring to a boil; reduce heat.
Simmer covered for 20 minutes or until potatoes are tender. Remove
stockpot from heat and mash potatoes; don't drain. In a small bowl,
blend one cup milk and flour until smooth. Add to potato mixture and
blend well. Add remaining milk and cheese, stir well. Cook over
medium heat until soup begins to thicken. Continue to cook and stir for
one minute. Add ham and parsley. Serves 4.

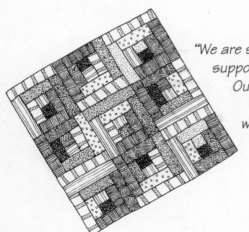

*"We are so grateful for the friendship and
support we've received over the years.
Our 15th Anniversary celebration
would not have been possible
without our families and all of our
Gooseberry Patch friends."*

Vickie
1999

Jalapeño-Cheese Soup

Marguerite Dearth
Circleville, OH

I think this soup is so yummy when the snow blows!

2 c. chicken broth
1 c. tomato, diced
1/4 t. garlic powder
2 potatoes, diced
6 T. butter
6 T. all-purpose flour
4 c. milk, divided

1/2 t. salt
pepper to taste
1 c. hot Monterey Jack cheese, grated
2 c. Monterey Jack cheese, grated
1/2 c. onion, finely chopped

In a stockpot, combine broth, tomato, garlic powder and potatoes. Heat to boiling; cover and reduce heat to medium. Simmer 10 minutes. Remove from heat; set aside. Melt butter in a saucepan, stir in flour and cook 3 minutes. Blend in 2-1/2 cups milk, 1/2 cup at a time, and continue to cook until smooth and thick. Remove from heat and stir into broth mixture. Return stockpot to stove and cook over medium heat. Stir in remaining milk, salt, pepper and cheese. Cook until cheese is melted and soup is thoroughly heated.

Dear Vickie & Jo Ann,

"I really enjoy your catalog because it's like my best friend dropping by and filling my hours with samples of original decorating ideas, unique homemade gifts and a feast of savory recipes! Thank you so much!"

Suzy Bridges
Hot Springs, AR

Jo Ann & Vickie pose with their Retail Entrepreneur of the Year awards -1995

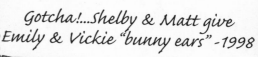

Gotcha!...Shelby & Matt give Emily & Vickie "bunny ears" -1998

Sydney helps her big brother Ryan get ready for a date -1998

Gooseberry Patch's biggest fans...Vickie's husband Shelby & Jo Ann's husband Jay -1990

Fresh-Picked Salads

Vickie, age 6, in her family's backyard garden.

Springtime Pasta Salad

Becky Svatora
Fremont, NE

This salad seems to be a hit everywhere I've taken it and I've been asked for the recipe several times! To make it even easier, just put the salad in a plastic container and shake...no need to stir.

16-oz. box spiral pasta, cooked
   and drained
2 t. salad oil
1-1/2 c. vinegar
1-1/2 c. sugar
1 t. salt
1 t. pepper

1 med. onion, chopped
1 cucumber, peeled and chopped
1 t. garlic salt
2 t. prepared mustard
2-oz. jar pimentos
1 T. parsley flakes

Coat pasta with salad oil; drain off excess. Combine remaining ingredients with pasta. Cover, and let marinate in refrigerator for 2 to 3 days before serving, stirring occasionally.

(1999)

Jo Ann & Vickie travel the country year-round looking for unique country collectibles to include in the next catalog. Some of their favorite items are Santas, candles, snowmen and cookie cutters.

Fresh-Picked Salads

Sunflower-Raspberry Salad

Donna Nowicki
Center City, MN

A great summertime salad! Sweet raspberries and crunchy apples are a perfect combination.

2 c. fresh raspberries
1 med. apple, diced
1 c. seedless green grapes,
   halved

1/2 c. celery, thinly sliced
1/4 c. raisins
1/2 c. raspberry yogurt
2 T. sunflower seeds, shelled

In a large bowl, combine first 5 ingredients. Stir yogurt in gently. Cover and refrigerate at least one hour. Add sunflower seeds just before serving.

Best-Ever Potato Salad

Judy Kelly
St. Charles, MO

This recipe was shared with me by a good friend. It's what we call a "foot-stompin'" good recipe! It's very rich and will wow your guests every time you serve it.

3-1/2 lbs. potatoes
1 qt. mayonnaise
3 T. vinegar

7 t. chicken bouillon granules
1 lb. bacon, crisply cooked and
   crumbled

Steam potatoes in skins until tender. Cool slightly and dice into one-inch cubes. Mix with mayonnaise, vinegar and bouillon; stir in bacon. Serve warm.

Ruby Coleslaw

Kerry Boyce
Katy, TX

The best coleslaw recipe and it's so pretty!

1 head red cabbage, thinly sliced
1 lg. red onion, finely sliced
3/4 c. plus 1 t. sugar, divided
1 c. cider vinegar

1-1/2 T. salt
2 t. celery seed
1 t. dry mustard
1-1/2 c. oil

In a large crock, alternate layers of cabbage and onion. Spread 3/4 cup of sugar on top; set aside. In a small saucepan, combine vinegar, salt, celery seed, mustard and remaining sugar. Bring mixture to a boil. Add oil and boil again. Pour over cabbage while hot. Cover tightly and refrigerate. Refrigerate for at least 6 hours, tossing periodically. Before serving, toss again. Makes 8 to 10 servings.

"As our Gooseberry Patch family has grown year after year, so have we! It's so much fun to look back on 15 years and see where we've come from. We started on a kitchen table and now we have our very own building in the country!"

Jo Ann
1999

Cucumber Salad

Diane Long
Gooseberry Patch

When I was a child, my grandmother would make this every Sunday to serve with chicken or roast beef, and on hot summer days, with hamburgers. Delicious!

2 lg. cucumbers, sliced
1 lg. sweet onion, sliced
2 T. cider vinegar

3 T. mayonnaise or sour cream
salt and pepper to taste
1/8 t. dried parsley

Combine all ingredients and refrigerate at least 2 hours to allow flavors to blend.

Blue Cheese Dressing

Janet Schaeper
Vickie's sister

Delicious as a salad dressing, dip for veggies or drizzled over a burger...so rich and flavorful!

1 pt. mayonnaise
1/4 c. lemon juice
1/4 T. garlic, minced
white pepper to taste

paprika to taste
1-1/4 lbs. sour cream
1 lb. crumbled blue cheese

Combine first 5 ingredients in large mixing bowl; blend for 2 minutes at low speed. Add sour cream and blue cheese; blend 4 minutes at low speed. Refrigerate 24 hours before serving.

Cranberry & Pineapple Salad

Debbie Austin
Corinth, TX

*My husband's grandmother gave me this recipe and asked me not to
tell anyone, but I feel it is a great tribute to her memory to share this
wonderful recipe. This is for you Grandma Richardson!*

12 oz. cranberries, finely
    chopped
1-1/2 c. sugar

1/2 c. crushed pineapple
2 3-oz. pkgs. strawberry gelatin
3 c. boiling water

Combine cranberries, sugar and pineapple. Mix well and let stand at
room temperature for 2 hours. Combine strawberry gelatin and water.
Let stand until cool, add to cranberry mixture. Pour into a 13"x9" pan.
Refrigerate until set.

Topping:

1 c. pineapple juice
1/2 c. sugar
1 egg yolk

2 T. all-purpose flour
2 T. butter
8 oz. whipped topping

Combine pineapple juice, sugar, egg yolk, flour and butter in medium
saucepan. Cook over medium heat until thickened. Remove from heat
and cool. Fold in whipped topping and spread over cranberry mixture.

The very first Gooseberry Patch catalog featured color photographs
of each product. To create a more "country-like feel" in their second
catalog, Vickie & Jo Ann traded in the photographs and began using
illustrated artwork instead...a tradition that still continues today!

Sweet Summer Salad

Angeline Haverstock
Portage, IN

Sesame seeds and toasted almonds give this salad crunch!

1/2 c. vegetable oil
1/4 c. sugar
2 T. vinegar
1 t. salt
1/4 t. pepper
1 lg. head iceberg lettuce,
   shredded

6 bacon slices, crisply cooked
   and crumbled
1/3 c. toasted almonds, sliced
2 T. sesame seeds
4 green onions, sliced
Garnish: 3/4 c. chow mein
   noodles

In a jar with a tight fitting lid, combine oil, sugar, vinegar, salt and pepper. Shake well. Refrigerate for at least 2 hours. Just before serving, combine the remaining ingredients. Top with the chow mein noodles, toss with dressing.

Ryan, Jay & Kyle enjoy
a dip in the ocean
-1992

Creamy Frozen Salad

Irene Robinson
Cincinnati, OH

This is a very refreshing salad for summer and so easy to make.

2 c. sour cream
2 T. lemon juice
3/4 c. sugar
1 banana, mashed

1/2 t. salt
9-oz. can crushed pineapple
1/4 c. maraschino cherries,
    chopped and drained

Blend sour cream, lemon juice and sugar; add banana. Stir in the remaining ingredients. Pour into a mold or muffin tins for individual servings. Place in freezer until frozen. Dip mold in warm water to loosen salad.

Walnut-Cranberry Salad

Kim Hunt
Washougal, WA

This was handed down from my grandmother. Mom made it for the holidays every year, now I make it for my family.

2 c. cranberries, ground
2 c. sugar
2 3-oz. pkgs. lemon gelatin

4 c. warm water
1 c. celery, diced
1 c. walnuts, chopped

Combine cranberries and sugar; let stand. Dissolve gelatin in water and chill until almost set. Fold in cranberries, celery and walnuts; chill.

Mailed in 1985, our first catalog was just 12 pages and featured 55 items. The catalog included 18 different patterns of homespun fabric and matching blue homespun dresses for mom and daughter!

Orange Sherbet Salad

Wanda Darnell
Littleton, CO

So cool and creamy! Serve it at your next summertime cook out!

3-oz. pkg. orange gelatin
1 c. boiling water
1/2 c. whipped cream
1/2 pt. orange sherbet, softened

1/2 c. mandarin oranges,
  drained
1/2 c. crushed pineapple,
  drained

Dissolve gelatin in boiling water and chill to egg white consistency. Whip with beater and fold in whipped cream. Add sherbet and remaining ingredients. Chill until ready to serve.

Dear Vickie & Jo Ann,

"I have just purchased my first Gooseberry Patch cookbook. I am looking forward to all those warm, wonderful aromas that will be wafting through my home soon."

Michelle Draves, Bay City, MI

Mexican Pasta Salad

Leslie Karr
Kansas City, MO

Use different shapes of pasta for variety. Twists and shells are pretty, as well as fun shapes like stars, hearts or patriotic flags.

8-oz. pkg. tricolor rotini, cooked and drained
15-oz. can kidney beans
8-oz. can whole kernel corn, drained
2 med. tomatoes, chopped

1 sm. green pepper, chopped
1/2 c. green onions, sliced
2-1/4 oz. can black olives, sliced
1 c. Mexican-blend cheese, shredded

In a large bowl, combine all salad ingredients; mix well and set aside.

Dressing:

10-oz. can diced tomatoes with green chilies

1/2 c. Italian dressing
2 t. herb seasoning

In a small bowl, combine ingredients. Pour over salad and toss to coat. Cover and chill until ready to serve.

Happy Birthday Grandma Tootsie!
Jo Ann's mom -1998

Fresh-Picked Salads

Red & Green Apple Salad

Betty McKay
Harmony, MN

This is a wonderful salad that is really good and very pretty. It's always a favorite at our house.

3 c. red and green apples, chopped
1 c. celery, thinly sliced
1 c. red grapes, halved

1/2 c. mayonnaise-type salad dressing
1/8 t. cinnamon
2 T. walnuts, chopped

Mix all ingredients except walnuts. Refrigerate. Add walnuts, and stir before serving.

Seven Layer Salad

DyAnn Sorensen
Virginia Beach, VA

My sister-in-law sent me this recipe about 15 years ago. My family loves it and whenever we have a potluck, I'm always asked to bring this. It's so easy because it can be made ahead of time.

1 head lettuce, torn
1 c. celery, diced
4 eggs, hard-boiled and chopped
15-1/4 oz. can peas, drained
1/2 c. green pepper, chopped

1 med. onion, finely chopped
2 c. mayonnaise
2 c. Cheddar cheese, shredded
6 bacon slices, crisply cooked and crumbled

In a large glass serving bowl, layer the first 6 ingredients beginning with lettuce and ending with onion. Spread mayonnaise over top layer; sprinkle with cheese and bacon. Refrigerate for at least 12 hours. Serves 10 to 12.

Crunchy Cabbage Salad

Phyllis Peters
Three Rivers, MI

In 1954, Bertha, a retired school teacher, was my neighbor. She made this recipe for church suppers and taught me to prepare this salad in an exact manner. Over the years it has been a family favorite. The other day I happened to meet up with an old friend and what did we mention with fond memories? Of course Bertha's cabbage salad and what a grand lady she proved to be to many housewives.

2 med. heads cabbage, shredded
1 green pepper, cut in strips
1 red pepper, cut in strips
3 lg. onions, sliced

1-1/2 c. sugar
3/4 c. white vinegar
3/4 c. vegetable oil
1 t. salt

In a very large bowl, place cabbage, peppers and onions. Heat the remaining ingredients in a saucepan, do not boil. Pour over the cabbage mix and let stand 2 hours to cool. Toss to mix thoroughly and refrigerate until ready to serve.

"The hardest part about running a business from your home was finding a place to store all the inventory. We had products lined up on shelves in the basement next to the power tools, golf clubs and boxes of old books!"

Jo Ann
1986

Spinach, Bacon & Apple Salad
Donna Nowicki
Center City, MN

Try a variety of apples; sweet Red Delicious, tart Granny Smith or spicy Fuji...they'll give your spinach salad a new taste each time.

1/4 c. olive oil
3 T. wine vinegar
1 t. sugar
1/2 t. prepared mustard
salt and pepper to taste
5 bacon slices, crisply cooked
    and crumbled, drippings
    reserved

1/3 c. almonds, sliced
1 lb. fresh spinach, torn
1 red apple, cored and coarsely
    chopped
3 green onions, thinly sliced

Combine first 4 ingredients with salt and pepper in a jar with a tight-fitting lid, shake well and refrigerate. Add one tablespoon reserved bacon fat and almonds to a skillet. Shake pan over medium-high heat until almonds are lightly toasted; remove from heat. In a large bowl, combine bacon, almonds, spinach, apple and onion; toss gently. Shake dressing and pour over salad. Toss well and serve immediately.

"Our kitchen tables were always covered with sample items, catalog pages, artwork, telephones and order sheets. Sometimes it was hard to tell the difference between dinner and Gooseberry Patch!"

Vickie
1990

Roasted Red Pepper Salad

Liz Plotnick
Gooseberry Patch

This salad's great for a seaside picnic; just pack up the kids and enjoy a day in the sun! Everyone will work up an appetite, so serve this with hearty club sandwiches and icy lemonade.

1 lb. red peppers
1/2 t. salt
1 T. lemon juice
1/2 c. olive oil
1 T. green onion, chopped

pepper to taste
1 to 2 bunches green leaf lettuce
1-1/2 lb. red new potatoes,
   cooked and sliced

Rinse peppers and slice off the top third; discard. Remove seeds and rinse inside of peppers thoroughly. Lightly oil a baking sheet and add peppers. Bake at 400 degrees for 15 minutes, or until peppers are tender. Dissolve 1/2 teaspoon salt in lemon juice; add olive oil, green onion and pepper; whisk until well blended; set aside. Layer leaf lettuce on a large serving dish; arrange potato slices on lettuce; top with roasted red pepper slices. Whisk dressing again and drizzle over salad. Serves 6.

Dear Vickie & Jo Ann,

"I want to tell you how much your books have meant to me these past two years, and encourage you to keep on writing! They're filled with so many heartwarming stories and suggestions! Thanks so much for sharing the positive and encouraging us to look for the good...and for your warm writing style and inspiration!"

Sherry Trimble, Cleveland, TN

Hawaiian Chicken Salad

Janice Tolifson
Alexandria, MN

A new twist on traditional chicken salad!

1 c. pasta, cooked and drained
1 to 2 chicken breasts, cooked
and cubed
11-oz. can mandarin oranges,
drained
1 c. mayonnaise-type salad
dressing

2 t. sugar
1 t. vinegar
1/4 to 1/2 c. cream or milk
Garnish: slivered almonds,
toasted coconut and
pineapple slices

Mix first 3 ingredients together; set aside. Prepare dressing by blending together mayonnaise, sugar, vinegar and enough cream or milk until dressing is of desired consistency. Toss salad with dressing to coat. Place in a serving bowl and sprinkle with almonds and coconut; top with pineapple slices.

Ryan, Robbie & Kyle building sand castles -1988

Asparagus & Tomato Salad
Barbara Rannazzisi
Elk Grove, CA

Fresh asparagus and tomatoes from your garden make this so great!

16 asparagus stalks
1 lb. Roma tomatoes, diced
1-1/2 T. fresh basil
1 t. salt

1/2 t. pepper
1/2 lb. Feta cheese, crumbled
1/3 c. balsamic vinegar

Cut the stems from asparagus stalks; discard. Slice asparagus on the diagonal and blanch in boiling water for 5 minutes. Remove from boiling water and immediately immerse in cold water to stop the cooking. In a large serving bowl, combine asparagus and tomatoes. Add basil, salt and pepper. Stir in Feta cheese; toss and refrigerate. Before serving, toss with balsamic vinegar.

Spicy Dressing
Helen Murray
Piketon, OH

Try this drizzled over fresh tomatoes, snow peas and avocado slices!

2 t. dry mustard
2 t. herb salt
2 t. paprika
1/4 c. sugar

1 lg. clove garlic, crushed
1 sm. onion, finely chopped
1/2 c. white wine vinegar
1 c. corn oil

Blend together well and refrigerate. Shake before serving. Toss with your favorite green salad.

Dear Vickie & Jo Ann,

"I am so thankful for such a wonderful collection of recipes! Each cookbook is so fun to read. I love to reminisce with people about their past; it brings back memories of my own!"

Anne Brown, Flushing, MI

Mother's Potato Salad

Helen Amstutz
Vickie's aunt

This is an old recipe handed down from my mother (Vickie's grandmother). She never had store-bought mayonnaise...this recipe made its own. We don't think potato salad made any other way tastes as good!

6 potatoes, peeled
3 celery stalks, chopped

1 med. onion, chopped
2 eggs, hard-boiled and chopped

Place potatoes in a saucepan and cover with water; boil until tender. Drain and let cool; cut into small cubes. Add celery, onion and eggs.

Dressing:

1 c. vinegar
1 c. water
1 T. butter
2 eggs, beaten
1 T. all-purpose flour

1/2 c. sugar
1/8 t. salt
mustard to taste
Garnish: paprika

Combine first 7 ingredients in a saucepan and cook until mixture begins to thicken. Stir in mustard, refrigerate until cool. Toss with potato mixture; sprinkle with paprika.

"My grandmother knew everything there was to know about feeding a large family. She made the best chicken & noodles, oyster dressing, strawberry-rhubarb pie, jams and jellies. When you'd ask for her recipe, she'd always answer 'It's just a pinch of this,' or 'a spoonful of that!'"

Vickie
1999

Pacific Coast Salad

Carol Koluncich
Santa Barbara, CA

This salad has become a family favorite and when we serve it for company, everyone wants the recipe. It is refreshing and delicious.

1 c. walnuts
2 T. butter, melted
seasoning salt to taste
1/2 head iceberg lettuce, torn
1/2 head romaine lettuce, torn
1 c. celery, chopped
1 med. red onion, thinly sliced
1/2 c. olive oil
2 T. red wine vinegar

1 T. lemon juice
1 clove garlic, halved
1 T. parsley, chopped
1 t. dry mustard
1/2 t. salt
1/8 t. pepper
3 t. sugar
2 c. oranges, sliced
2 avocados, sliced

Stir walnuts with butter; add seasoning salt. Spread on a cookie sheet and bake at 400 degrees for 10 minutes; stir occasionally. Remove from oven; set aside to cool. In a large serving bowl, combine lettuce, celery and onion. Mix remaining ingredients, except oranges and avocados, in a bottle with a tight fitting lid; shake well. Pour over salad ingredients. Toss lightly. Top with walnuts, oranges and avocados. Serves 8.

Matt at Lake Erie -1987

Sauerkraut Salad

Cindy Watson
Gooseberry Patch

This recipe is a family favorite given to me by my grandpa.

1 qt. sauerkraut, rinsed and
    drained
1 green pepper, chopped
1 sm. onion, chopped
2/3 c. celery, chopped

1-1/2 c. sugar
1/4 c. oil
2/3 c. vinegar
1/3 c. water

Combine sauerkraut, green pepper, onion and celery; mix well. In a separate bowl, blend together remaining ingredients; pour over sauerkraut mixture. Refrigerate overnight before serving.

Cheesy Broccoli Salad

Gail Banasiak
Dayton, OH

For variety try Muenster, hot pepper or Provolone cheeses!

2 c. broccoli flowerets, partially
    cooked
2 c. mushrooms, sliced
1/2 c. buttermilk salad dressing

2 c. red cabbage, chopped
2 oz. Colby cheese, cubed
2 oz. Swiss cheese, cubed
1 c. cherry tomatoes, halved

Combine broccoli and mushrooms with salad dressing; toss. Cover and refrigerate at least 2 hours to blend. Toss before serving with remaining ingredients. Makes 5 servings.

Oriental Salad

Cheryl Hambleton
Gooseberry Patch

I made this for a Gooseberry Patch cookout last summer and it was a hit! Now I'm asked to bring it every time we get together.

2 pkgs. beef ramen noodles, crumbled
3/4 c. sunflower seeds, toasted
3/4 c. almonds, slivered
2 T. butter, melted
16-oz. pkg. shredded cabbage
1/2 c. onion, chopped
1/2 c. radish, chopped
1/2 c. green pepper, chopped
1 c. safflower oil
1/3 c. vinegar
1/2 c. sugar
2 T. soy sauce
2 beef flavor packets from ramen noodles

Spread ramen noodles, sunflower seeds, almonds and butter on cookie sheet. Bake at 350 degrees for 15 minutes or until brown. Let cool. In a large bowl, place ramen noodle mixture, cabbage, onion, radish and green pepper. In medium bowl, combine safflower oil, vinegar, sugar, soy sauce and beef packets; shake well. Thirty minutes prior to serving, add dressing. Serve well chilled.

When Vickie & Jo Ann met over their backyard fence 15 years ago, they had no idea their love for country decorating and antiques would inspire them to create their very own business.

Harvest Spinach Salad

Barb Bargdill
Gooseberry Patch

We love to go apple picking in the autumn and try to include apples in everything from main courses to salads and desserts. This is one of our favorite salads.

1 bunch fresh spinach, washed, dried and stems removed
5 bacon slices, crisply cooked and crumbled
5 green onions, sliced
1/2 c. almonds, sliced
1 Red Delicious apple, thinly sliced

1/2 c. Monterey Jack cheese, cubed
1/4 c. olive oil
3 T. white wine vinegar
1 t. sugar
1/2 t. dry mustard

Toss together spinach, bacon, green onions, almonds, apple and cheese. In a small bowl, combine olive oil, vinegar, sugar and mustard; shake. Toss dressing with salad.

"Back when we first started Gooseberry Patch, we'd load the old family van full of our Gooseberry goodies and hit the open road on the weekends! Vickie and I would travel around Ohio to different craft and antique shows, marketing our wares to just about anyone who was interested. We made a lot of new friends that way...friends we still keep in touch with today!"

Jo Ann
1988

Strawberry-Pretzel Salad

Corrine Lane
Gooseberry Patch

Growing up I wasn't much help to my mother in the kitchen; I always had an excuse to get out of cooking! When I married my high school sweetheart, one of our first agreements was he would cook and I'd do the dishes; this still holds after 11 years of marriage. Over time; however, I decided to find recipes I could make with ease. This salad is one of the best recipes I've found.

2 c. salted pretzels, crushed
1/2 c. butter, melted
3 T. plus 1 c. sugar, divided
8-oz. pkg. cream cheese, softened

12 oz. whipped topping
3-oz. pkg. strawberry gelatin
2 c. boiling water
2 10-oz. pkgs. frozen strawberries, thawed

Mix together pretzels, butter and 3 tablespoons sugar. Press in the bottom of 13"x9" baking pan. Bake at 375 degrees for 8 minutes; let cool. Beat cream cheese and sugar; add whipped topping. Spread over cooled crust and refrigerate 10 to 15 minutes. Dissolve gelatin in boiling water, add strawberries and mix well. Let stand 10 to 15 minutes and pour over cheese layer. Refrigerate until ready to serve.

1991

Brenda Warne from Rockford, MI, was the winner of the very first Gooseberry Patch recipe contest. Brenda entered a recipe for "Cinnamon Sheep" cookies, a copy of which was mailed with every cookie cutter order from the Holiday 1991 catalog.

Refreshing Fruit Salad

Teri Lindquist
Gurnee, IL

This beautiful salad is my absolute favorite. You can prepare it quickly and the colors are a feast for the eyes! This is a recipe you'll want to make often.

1 c. strawberries, sliced
1 c. green grapes, halved
11-oz. can mandarin oranges, drained
20-oz. can pineapple tidbits, drained, juice reserved

1 c. blueberries
1/4 c. honey
1/4 c. lemon juice

Combine strawberries, grapes, oranges, pineapple and blueberries in a mixing bowl. In a separate bowl, whisk together honey, lemon juice and 1/4 cup reserved pineapple juice. Toss gently with fruit. Cover and refrigerate several hours or overnight. Serves 4 to 6.

"We've made our share of mistakes over the years! Like the time when the covers for two of our catalogs were supposed to be Williamsburg blue and barn red...two great country colors, right? Well, they turned out gray and rust instead. It wasn't funny then, but we can look back now and laugh!"

Vickie
1999

Malibu Greens Salad

Chris Kelley
Delaware, OH

A wonderful salad served with warm bread and garlic dipping oil.

12 c. mixed baby greens
2 c. carrot strips, shredded
1/4 c. orange juice concentrate
1/4 c. sherry wine vinegar
1/4 c. honey
1/4 c. Dijon mustard

2 T. roasted garlic purée
3/4 t. salt
3/4 t. pepper
1 c. olive oil
Garnish: 1/4 c. toasted cashews
    and 1/4 c. dried cranberries

Place the mixed baby greens and carrot strips in a mixing bowl; set aside. Combine orange juice concentrate, sherry wine vinegar, honey, Dijon mustard, roasted garlic, salt and pepper in a stainless steel bowl and whisk until well blended. Continue to whisk while adding olive oil. Garnish each serving with cashews and cranberries. Makes 8 servings.

Creamy Garlic Dressing

Debby Sprechman
Miramar, FL

Nothing's as fresh as homemade salad dressing!

1 c. mayonnaise
1/4 c. sour cream
1-1/2 t. garlic powder
1 t. pepper

1/4 c. olive oil
1 T. sugar
1 t. vinegar
1/4 c. skim milk

Combine all ingredients together until well blended. Refrigerate at least one hour to allow flavors to blend. Toss with your favorite green salad. Serves 24.

Fresh-Picked Salads

Summertime Carrot Salad
Wendy Paffenroth
Pine Island, NY

Carrot salad is a recipe that's been handed down from my great-aunt Elsie. Her son kindly gave me all of her recipes, some hardly readable today. It is so nice to see her handwriting and know that she too liked to create in the kitchen.

6 c. carrots, sliced
1 lg. onion, sliced
1 lg. green pepper, chopped
10-3/4 oz. can tomato soup
3/4 c. sugar

1 c. oil
3/4 c. vinegar
1 t. salt
1 t. dry mustard
pepper to taste

Cook carrots in boiling water until tender; drain and cool. Place in a bowl with onion and green pepper. Blend the remaining ingredients together well and pour over carrot mixture. Cover and refrigerate 24 hours before serving.

Jo Ann & Vickie pose for a quick photo beside Vickie's big red barn -1997

Italian Salad

Kathy Grashoff
Ft. Wayne, IN

*The perfect side salad for any family dinner. Try it
with lasagna and warm homemade rolls.*

1-1/2 lbs. broccoli, chopped
2-1/4 c. Swiss cheese, shredded
3-1/2 oz. pkg. sliced pepperoni

3-oz. can green or black olives,
   sliced
.7-oz. pkg. dry Italian dressing

In serving bowl, toss broccoli with Swiss cheese, pepperoni and olives.
Prepare Italian dressing according to package directions. Just before
serving, pour dressing over salad; toss to coat evenly.

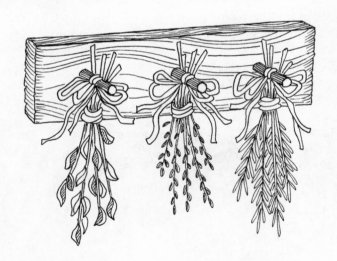

Dear Vickie & Jo Ann,

"What a thrill to have one of our family recipes included in "Family
Favorites"! The recipes are tried-and-true and are quick and easy to
prepare. I will treasure my copy of this special book. Thank you!"

Joan Morris, Tallahassee, FL

Black Bean Salad

Robbin Chamberlain
Gooseberry Patch

*I usually think of this as a springtime salad because it's so
colorful. Very yummy if you're a cilantro fan, like me!*

1 T. sugar
1 T. lime zest
6 T. lime juice
4 t. cumin
1-1/2 t. salt
3/4 c. olive oil
1 c. yellow pepper, chopped
3 jalapeño peppers, seeded and
    finely chopped
1 c. red onion, chopped

1 c. celery, diced
1/2 c. fresh cilantro, chopped
4 15-oz. cans black beans,
    rinsed and drained
3 avocados, chopped
2 c. plum tomatoes, chopped
salt to taste
pepper to taste
Boston or romaine lettuce

Prepare dressing by combining sugar, lime zest and lime juice; stir until sugar is dissolved. Add cumin and salt. Whisk in olive oil. Cover and set aside while preparing salad. In a large serving bowl, combine yellow pepper, jalapeños, onion, celery, cilantro and beans; mixing well. Pour in dressing and toss to coat. Gently stir in avocados and tomatoes; add salt and pepper. Cover and refrigerate 2 to 5 hours. Bring to room temperature before serving. Line serving bowl with lettuce, spoon prepared salad on top.

"We read everything we could get our hands on about the mail order business until finally, our first catalog was mailed in August 1985. Five years later, our goals remain the same. We are still operating from our homes, and bulging at the seams, working with wonderful employees and still feeling that same excitement and dedication we felt in the beginning."

Vickie
1989

Family Reunion Macaroni Salad

Jan Jolley
Elyria, OH

*Slightly sweet and creamy, this salad can be made
ahead of time; up to a week before serving.*

1 lb. twist macaroni
2 c. green pepper, chopped
1-1/2 c. carrots, chopped
1 c. onion, chopped
1 pt. mayonnaise

14-oz. can sweetened
   condensed milk
1 c. sugar
1 c. vinegar

Cook macaroni according to package directions; drain and refrigerate to
cool. Combine remaining ingredients with macaroni, mix well to blend.

Mother-Daughter moment -July 1998

"Every summer we host a family party at our house. It's a day of sun
and fun...a family potluck where everyone brings their favorite dish.
Here I am with my mom, my sister Janet and my great-niece, Briana.
It's a special day...sharing food, laughter and memories."

Vickie
1998

German Potato Salad

Robyn Wright
Gooseberry Patch Artisan

This is a family recipe from Wisconsin...excellent!

4 to 5 lbs. potatoes
1 lb. bacon, diced
1 med. onion, diced
1 c. plus 1/4 c. water, divided

1 c. sugar
2/3 c. white vinegar
1 T. cornstarch

Boil potatoes until tender. Cool slightly, peel and slice into bite-size pieces. Fry bacon until nearly crisp, add onion and continue to cook until bacon becomes crisp and onion is tender; remove from saucepan. Drain all but 1/4 cup drippings from saucepan; set aside. In a small bowl, combine one cup water, sugar and vinegar. Add to reserved drippings in skillet; heat to boiling. Combine 1/4 cup water with cornstarch, mixing well, blend into sugar mixture. Cook until thick, stir in potatoes, bacon and onion; mix well.

Honey-Mustard Dressing

Joanne West
Beavercreek, OH

For a different taste, try teriyaki or white wine mustard!

1/2 c. honey
1-1/2 c. mayonnaise

1/4 c. Dijon mustard

In a medium bowl, whisk all ingredients together until well blended.

1991

After receiving more than 800 recipes and letters of encouragement from Gooseberry Patch friends and customers, Jo Ann & Vickie began work on their very first cookbook in late 1991.

Ida's Sawdust Salad

Milly Doerr
Manassas, VA

This is a recipe Mom took everywhere; it was just expected. When she passed away, everyone asked if I would carry on the tradition, but I didn't have the recipe. While cleaning out a storage room in my parents' house one day, I found the recipe on a card, in Mom's handwriting, laying on the floor...it was as if she'd sent it to me.

6-oz. pkg. lemon gelatin
6-oz. pkg. orange gelatin
2 c. boiling water
2 c. cold water
20-oz. can of crushed pineapple
4 to 6 bananas, sliced

1-lb. bag of mini-marshmallows
3 c. pineapple juice
1 c. water
1 c. sugar
4 to 6 T. all-purpose flour

In large casserole dish, combine both flavors of gelatin with hot water; stir until gelatin is dissolved. Blend in cold water, pineapple, bananas and mini-marshmallows. Cover tightly and refrigerate for at least one hour or until jelled. In a blender, combine pineapple juice, water, sugar and flour. Blend on high for 2 minutes. Pour the liquid into a heavy saucepan and cook over medium heat to boiling. Continue to boil mixture over medium-low for 10 minutes, or until it thickens to the consistency of pudding. Let the mixture cool to room temperature and then pour it over the chilled gelatin mixture. Return to the refrigerator, covered tightly, for several hours or overnight.

Topping:

1 envelope whipped topping mix
2 8-oz. pkgs. cream cheese, softened

Garnish: 14-oz. bag of shredded coconut

Make whipped topping according to directions on the box. Gradually add the cream cheese, a little at a time, until the topping is smooth and creamy. Spread the topping over the second layer of the salad and garnish with the coconut. Serves 10 to 15.

Granny Smith Salad

Dorothy Foor
Jeromesville, OH

Tangy and crisp...a nice change!

1/4 c. lime juice
1 T. Dijon mustard
salt and pepper to taste
3/4 c. olive oil
4 Granny Smith apples, cored
    and chopped

1/2 c. green onions, thinly sliced
2 c. cranberries, chopped
1/4 c. sugar
2 c. red leaf lettuce

Combine lime juice, Dijon mustard and salt and pepper in a medium bowl; whisk until well blended. While whisking, add olive oil a little at a time. In a separate bowl with a tight fitting lid, combine apple and onions; toss with olive oil mixture. Refrigerate 3 hours. Combine cranberries and sugar; mixing well. Cover and refrigerate 2 hours. Before serving, line individual plates with red leaf lettuce, spoon on cranberry mixture. Serves 8.

Sydney loves
getting hugs
from her big
brothers Robbie
& Kyle
-1998

Ryan makes a new
friend at the zoo -1989

Jo Ann & Ryan
-1984

Welcome to the family,
Sport! -1992

Bread Basket

Vickie, age 4, Easter morning

Golden Butter Rolls

Susan Ingersoll
Gooseberry Patch Artisan

I'm very blessed to have a wonderful mom; and doubly blessed that she's also a great cook. This recipe may seem like a lot of work, but it's well worth the effort. Our entire family loves these delicious rolls!

1 c. milk
1 stick plus 1/2 c. butter
1 pkg. active dry yeast
1/2 c. plus 1 t. sugar, divided
1/2 c. lukewarm water

1 t. salt
3 eggs, beaten
1 c. whole wheat flour
3-1/2 to 4 cups all-purpose flour

In a heavy saucepan, scald milk and butter. Remove from heat and cool. In a small bowl, dissolve yeast and one teaspoon sugar in luke-warm water. When mixture foams, add to a large mixing bowl with remaining sugar, salt, eggs, whole wheat and all-purpose flour. Add the cooled milk mixture and mix until smooth. Knead on a lightly floured board until shiny, then place in a large oiled bowl; brush the top of dough with soft butter. Cover and let dough rise until double in size. Divide dough into 3 portions. Using a rolling pin, roll each portion in a 1/2-inch thick circle. Cut each circle into 10 or 12 pie-shaped wedges. Roll each up from the large end and place one inch apart on a greased cookie sheet. Repeat with remaining portions of dough. Brush the tops of each roll with softened butter; let rise until double. Bake at 375 degrees for 15 to 20 minutes or until golden. Remove and brush with butter while rolls are still warm.

Whole Wheat Bread

Diann Fox
Lewisberry, PA

A woman in our church has been making this bread for us for more years than I am allowed to mention! It's delicious and easy to make.

3 c. warm water
3 pkgs. active dry yeast
1/4 c. honey
5 c. whole wheat flour

5 t. salt
5 c. all-purpose flour
5 T. oil

Mix together water, yeast and honey. Add whole wheat flour and salt; mix well. Stir in all-purpose flour. Pour oil over the dough and knead 2 to 3 minutes. Cover dough and let rise for 45 minutes. Punch down and knead slightly. Shape into 2 loaves and place in greased loaf pans. Let rise until double in size. Bake at 400 degrees for 20 minutes, then loosely cover with a tent of aluminum foil. Bake 10 minutes longer. Makes 2 loaves.

"There really were some tight growing pains when we moved Gooseberry Patch out of our houses and into a small office in 1989. We had to do a lot of different 'jobs' to make the business work. Vickie was busy writing catalog copy and I'd be out front unloading new inventory from a truck. We did whatever we had to do in those days; we each wore many different hats."

Jo Ann
1999

Country Cornbread

Missy Collier
Buellton, CA

You can leave out the jalapeño and still have a terrific country-style cornbread, but you really should try it with the pepper! Either way it's great served with a bowl of chili or homemade stew.

1-1/4 c. cornmeal
3/4 c. all-purpose flour
5 T. sugar
2 t. baking powder
1/2 t. salt
1 c. buttermilk
1/3 c. vegetable oil

1 lg. egg, lightly beaten
1 c. sharp Cheddar cheese, grated
1 c. corn kernels
1 T. fresh jalapeño, seeded and minced

In a large bowl, mix together cornmeal, flour, sugar, baking powder and salt. Make a well in the center of the mix and pour in it the buttermilk, oil and egg. Stir lightly until ingredients are lightly moistened. Fold in cheese, corn and jalapeño; stir. Pour mixture into lightly oiled 8"x8" baking dish. Bake at 375 degrees for 25 to 30 minutes, or until a tester inserted in the center comes out clean. Let cool slightly, cut into squares.

Little prairie girl Emily all dressed up in homespun!
-1987

Bread Basket

Quick Cheddar Bread

Carolyn Graves
Moselle, MS

You won't have to wait long for warm bread when you use this recipe.

2 c. all-purpose flour
1 T. sugar
1 T. baking powder
1/2 t. salt
1/4 c. butter

3/4 c. milk
1 egg
1 c. sharp Cheddar cheese,
   shredded

Coat a 8"x4" loaf pan with non-stick cooking spray; set aside. Stir flour, sugar, baking powder and salt together. Cut in butter until mixture resembles coarse crumbs. Stir milk and egg into flour mixture; add Cheddar cheese. Stir well and pour batter into prepared pan. Bake at 350 degrees for 35 minutes or until golden brown.

Garlic Butter Spread

Heather Alexander
Lacey, WV

Delicious on grilled or broiled bread.

1 stick butter, softened
2 cloves garlic, crushed

1 t. Italian seasoning
1/4 t. salt

Mix ingredients, refrigerate overnight to blend.

Dear Vickie & Jo Ann,

"My first package from you just arrived! The beautiful aroma of apple and cinnamon greeted me when I opened the parcel and just looking through your catalog makes my heart warm! Thank you so much for sharing all your lovely country stuff with me."

Eri Noda, London, England

Grammie's Cinnies

Laurie Williams
Gooseberry Patch Artisan

Being a city girl moving from California to Ohio, many of my friends said it couldn't be done. Several teased that I'd fit in so well I'd win ribbons in the county fair. Not one to ignore a challenge, I entered my grandmother's cinnamon rolls in the county fair. Well, I showed them that a city girl could adapt! I won a blue ribbon...for the cinnamon rolls and for my grandmother!

1-1/2 c. scalded milk
1 c. sugar
2 cakes compressed yeast
6 c. all-purpose flour, divided
4 eggs

1/2 t. salt
1 to 2 c. butter, divided
cinnamon
brown sugar

In a large bowl, pour milk over sugar; stir. When milk has cooled to lukewarm, crumble yeast cakes and dissolve in milk. Stir in 3 cups flour; mix well. Let rise until bubbles form, about 45 minutes. Beat eggs with salt and one cup butter; add to yeast mixture. Cover and let rise 1-1/2 hours. Remove dough to a lightly floured surface, knead with as much additional flour as needed until dough has a silky feel and is no longer sticky. Divide dough in half and shape to resemble a loaf of French bread. Roll dough into a rectangle, 1/3-inch thick and 10 inches long. Spread dough with as much butter, cinnamon and brown sugar as desired. Beginning at the long end, roll the dough tightly. Cut the dough into 1-1/2 inch rolls and place one inch apart on lightly oiled pans. Let rolls rise 30 minutes. Repeat with remaining half of dough. Bake at 400 degrees for 20 minutes or until lightly golden.

"My favorite part of the business is coming up with ideas for products, books, catalogs and newsletters. It's amazing how creative we can get over chocolate chip cookies and M&M®'s!"

Vickie
1999

Lemon Bread

Wendy Paffenroth
Pine Island, NY

*The lemon gives this bread a refreshing taste. Enjoy it warm
with a cup of herbal tea, or cold with fresh strawberries.*

1 c. shortening
2 c. plus 1/2 c. sugar, divided
4 lg. eggs, beaten
3 c. all-purpose flour
1/2 t. salt

2 t. baking powder
8 oz. lemon yogurt
juice of 1 lemon, divided
1 T. lemon zest

Preheat oven to 350 degrees. Grease two 8" loaf pans. Cream the
shortening and 2 cups sugar; add eggs and mix well. Sift the flour, salt
and baking powder and add alternately with the yogurt mixture to
the creamed mixture. Blend 1/2 of the lemon juice and the zest into
the mixture. Divide the mixture evenly into each loaf pan and bake
45 to 55 minutes. A toothpick inserted in the center should come out
clean when bread is done. Combine remaining sugar and lemon juice
together. While bread is still hot, drizzle over the top.

*"Vickie and I want to create great
cookbooks with simple recipes for
people who love to spend time in the
kitchen, but have busy family
lives with kids and dogs and cats,
a home to care for and a job
to do...basically, a cookbook for
everyone just like us!"*

Jo Ann
1995

Monkey Bread

*Beth Hall
Rochester Hills, MI*

*I've loved this bread for as long as I can remember, now my own
kids enjoy it, too. While it's baking, the aroma of cinnamon
and sugar fills the kitchen.*

3 12-oz. tubes biscuits
1/2 c. sugar
2 t. cinnamon, divided

1 stick of butter
1 c. brown sugar, packed

Cut biscuits in quarters. Mix together sugar and one teaspoon
cinnamon. Roll each biscuit piece in sugar and cinnamon mixture.
Place in a Bundt® pan. In saucepan, heat butter, brown sugar and
remaining cinnamon. Pour over biscuits. Bake at 350 degrees for 30
minutes. Turn over onto a plate and let stand for 10 minutes.

Pecan Butter

*MaryAnn Fearby
Medina, NY*

I love this nutty spread on toast or muffins.

2 c. pecans, finely chopped
1 c. butter, softened

1/2 c. powdered sugar

Combine all ingredients in a bowl until well blended and creamy. Store
in refrigerator until ready to serve. Makes 2 cups.

Bread Basket

Rise 'n Shine Orange Bread

Linda Brown
Severn, MD

A burst of cranberry and orange flavors make a great combination!

3 c. all-purpose flour
3/4 c. sugar
1 T. baking powder
1 t. salt
1/2 t. baking soda

1 c. orange juice
1/2 c. butter, melted
2 eggs, beaten
1-1/4 c. cranberries, chopped
1/2 c. nuts, chopped

Oil a 9-1/4"x5-1/4" loaf pan; set aside. Mix together flour, sugar, baking powder, salt and baking soda. Combine orange juice, butter and eggs; stir into dry ingredients mixing until just moistened. Blend in cranberries and nuts. Spoon mixture into prepared pan and bake at 350 degrees for one hour and 5 minutes or until toothpick inserted into loaf comes out clean. Bake for 5 more minutes, then remove from pans and cool on cooling rack.

Sydney's first family vacation -1996

"We took 15-month-old Sydney on her first family Christmas vacation shortly after we brought her home from Russia. She just loved playing in the sunshine, running through the sand and dipping her toes in the ocean. After opening all our presents, everyone agreed...Sydney was the best gift of all!"

Jo Ann
1996

Cheddar Shortbread

Robin Sager
Hardin, KY

For a tasty variation, add sun-dried tomatoes and minced garlic.

2 c. sharp Cheddar cheese,
   shredded
1-1/2 c. all-purpose flour
3/4 t. dry mustard

1/4 t. cayenne pepper
1/2 c. butter, melted
1 T. water, optional

Toss dry ingredients together; mix in butter. Mix with your hands to form a dough. Add water if dough feels too dry. On a floured surface, roll out half the dough 1/8-inch to 1/4-inch thick. Cut with cookie cutters and place on ungreased cookie sheet. Repeat with the remaining dough. Bake at 375 degrees for 10 to 12 minutes. Remove to rack to cool.

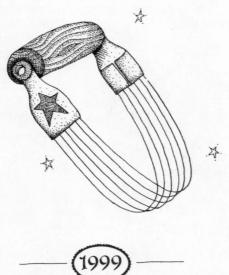

1999

Designing the Gooseberry Patch catalog is a year-round project for Vickie & Jo Ann. Production for the annual Holiday catalog begins just after Christmas, while the Spring catalog starts in July.

Oatmeal Bread

Betty Richer
Grand Junction, CO

Growing up, this bread was made several times a month in our home. In later years, I lived 40 miles from my folks, but they would call on Sunday afternoons and lure me out to the big house on the river for soup and homemade oatmeal bread.

1 pkg. active dry yeast
2 c. lukewarm water
10 c. all-purpose flour, divided
2 c. oatmeal
1/2 c. molasses

1/2 c. brown sugar, packed
1 T. salt
1 T. shortening
2 c. boiling water

Dissolve yeast in lukewarm water. Add 2 cups of flour; consistency will be spongy. Let dough rise one hour. In a separate bowl combine oatmeal, molasses, brown sugar, salt and shortening. Pour molasses mixture into boiling water, stir and cool. After yeast has risen, pour into molasses mixture. Add remaining 8 cups of flour; mixing well. Let dough rise until double in size. Lightly knead and divide into 4 sections. Shape 3 sections into loaves and place into 3 oiled 9" loaf pans. Shape remaining section into rolls and place in a lightly oiled 8"x8" baking pan. Bake at 375 degrees for 45 to 50 minutes. Makes one pan of rolls and 3 loaves of bread.

"Matt and Ryan ride their bicycles into town to come help out at Gooseberry Patch after school. They'll pack boxes, clean the windows in the front office and sweep the sidewalk... or at least until they have enough quarters to run across the street for ice cream and candy."

Vickie
1990

Sunflower-Vegetable Bread

Vickie

This bread is delicious with soup or sliced for sandwiches.

2 T. active dry yeast
1/2 c. warm water
4 c. milk
1/4 c. sugar
4 t. salt
1/4 c. butter
3 eggs, beaten
11-1/2 to 12-1/2 c. all-purpose
    flour, divided
1/2 c. red cabbage, finely
    chopped

1/2 c. onions, finely chopped
1/3 c. celery, finely chopped
1/4 c. green pepper, finely
    chopped
1/4 c. cucumber, peeled, seeded
    and finely chopped
1 clove garlic, finely minced
3/4 c. carrots, grated
Garnish: 1/2 c. sunflower seeds,
    divided

Combine yeast and warm water; allow yeast to dissolve completely.
Mix together milk, sugar, salt, butter, eggs and 6 cups of flour; add
yeast mixture. Stir in remaining vegetables and enough flour to make a
soft dough; knead 5 minutes. Let rise in a warm place until double in
size. Punch down and let rise again. Divide dough into quarters; shape
into loaves. Place loaves in 4 greased 8-1/2"x4-1/2" loaf pans.
Sprinkle sunflower seeds evenly over each loaf; cover and let dough
rise until double in size. Bake at 375 degrees for 35 to 40 minutes.
Makes 4 loaves.

*We stumbled on
this beautiful
sunflower patch
and just had to
stop for a photo!
-1993*

Bread Basket

Easy Orange Rolls

Robyn Wright
Gooseberry Patch Artisan

So easy to make and what a wonderful aroma while they're baking!

1/2 c. butter
3/4 c. sugar
2 T. frozen orange juice

zest of 2 oranges
3 12-oz. tubes of biscuits

In a small saucepan, combine butter and sugar. Heat until sugar dissolves. Blend in frozen orange juice and orange zest. Open each tube of biscuits and separate. Dip individual biscuits in orange mixture and layer in a lightly oiled Bundt® pan; repeat with all biscuits. Pour any remaining orange mixture over biscuits. Bake at 375 degrees for 20 minutes.

Honey-Lemon Glaze

Gail Banasiak
Dayton, OH

This glaze is wonderful drizzled over rolls, muffins or warm bread.

1/2 t. lemon zest
1/2 c. honey

1 t. lemon juice
powdered sugar

Blend lemon zest, honey and lemon juice together. Add enough powdered sugar until desired consistency is reached.

"Here at Gooseberry Patch we start each morning with a smile and set our priorities...it may be collecting artwork for the next catalog, selecting new products, heading out on a buying trip or brainstorming for a new cookbook. The best part is working alongside so many dedicated, talented people who make "going to work" fun!"

Vickie
1988

Dill Bread

Lori White
Cairo, MO

When I was a little girl, I would often spend the night with my grandparents. My grandma and I would always be in the kitchen cooking; she even made me my own little apron to wear. This is a recipe we made often.

1 pkg. active dry yeast
1/4 c. warm water
1 c. cottage cheese, warmed
2 T. sugar
1 T. onion, minced
1 T. butter

2 t. dill seed
1 t. salt
1/4 t. baking soda
1 egg
2-1/4 to 2-1/2 c. all-purpose
   flour

Soften yeast in water; set aside. Combine next 8 ingredients; add in yeast mixture and enough flour to make a stiff dough. Cover, let rise until double, punch down. Shape and place in a 2-quart casserole. Let rise again, 30 to 40 minutes. Bake at 350 degrees for 40 to 50 minutes or until brown. Makes 10 to 15 servings.

"Potlucks have recently become a big part of working at Gooseberry Patch. As we've grown over the years, our potlucks have become more like feasts, with everyone bringing their favorite dishes, and recipes, to share!"

Jo Ann
1999

Parmesan Bread

Barbara Arnold
Toledo, OH

Perfect for any Italian dish!

1 pkg. active dry yeast
1 c. warm water
3 c. all-purpose flour, divided
1/2 c. butter, divided
1 egg, beaten
2 T. sugar

1 t. salt
1-1/2 t. dried minced onion
1/2 t. Italian seasoning
1/2 t. garlic salt
1/2 c. grated Parmesan cheese,
    divided

Dissolve yeast in warm water. Add 2 cups flour, 1/4 cup softened butter, egg, sugar, salt and seasonings. Beat at low speed until well blended. Increase mixer speed to medium and continue to beat 2 minutes longer. Stir in remaining flour and 1/3 cup cheese; beat until smooth. Cover dough and let rise one hour, or until double in size. Using a wooden spoon, stir dough 25 times. Melt remaining butter; set aside. Spread batter in an oiled 1-1/2 quart casserole dish, top with melted butter and sprinkle remaining cheese over top. Cover and let rise 30 minutes. Bake at 350 degrees for 35 minutes or until golden. Cool on wire rack 10 minutes before removing from casserole dish.

"Success didn't come easily at first. One lesson Jo Ann and I learned early was to fill the Gooseberry Patch catalog with items our customers liked...not just what we liked. I remember the time we both fell in love with this museum-quality plate. We put it in the catalog and sold just two...guess who bought them?"

Vickie
1997

Gracie's Banana Nut Bread

Debbie Dye
Gooseberry Patch

My Aunt Gracie shared this old family recipe with me. I like to bake it in small loaf pans to share with my neighbors.

1 stick butter
1-1/2 c. sugar
2 eggs
1 t. vanilla extract
2 to 3 sm. bananas, mashed

2 c. all-purpose flour
1 t. baking soda
3/4 t. salt
1/2 c. sour cream
1 c. walnuts, chopped

Cream butter and sugar. Add eggs and vanilla; beat well. Mix in bananas. In a separate bowl, combine flour, baking soda and salt. Add alternately to the butter mixture with the sour cream. Fold in nuts and stir. Pour batter into an oiled 9"x4" loaf pan. Bake at 350 degrees for one hour, or until toothpick inserted in the center comes out clean.

Bee Bread

Linda Speer
Fort Scott, KS

Watch as your family makes a bee-line for these!

1 c. corn syrup
1-1/2 c. powdered sugar,
    divided

1 c. peanut butter
1-1/4 c. powdered milk

Combine corn syrup, 1-1/4 cups powdered sugar, peanut butter and powdered milk. Roll mixture into 1 to 2-inch balls and then roll in remaining powdered sugar so that bread is not sticky.

Bread Basket

Little Angel Biscuits

Terri Demidovich
Charleston, SC

*Great for breakfast with honey on top, or served with
sausage gravy for a hearty farmhouse breakfast!*

1 pkg. active dry yeast
1/4 c. warm water
3-1/2 to 4 c. all-purpose flour,
    divided
1/2 t. baking soda
2 t. baking powder

1/2 t. salt
1/4 c. sugar
1/2 c. shortening
1 c. buttermilk
1 egg, beaten

Dissolve yeast in warm water; set aside. In a separate bowl, combine
3-1/2 cups flour with remaining dry ingredients; cut in shortening.
Blend in buttermilk, egg and yeast mixture. Turn on a lightly floured
surface and knead lightly. Add any additional flour as needed to keep
dough from being too sticky. Roll out to 1/2-inch thick and cut with a
biscuit cutter. Place on a lightly oiled baking sheet and let dough sit for
10 minutes. Bake at 400 degrees for 12 to 15 minutes or until lightly
golden. Makes 24 biscuits.

*Emily's ready to hit the road on her
brother's 3-wheeler -1982*

Fresh Strawberry Muffins

Kathy Grashoff
Ft. Wayne, IN

Begin your own strawberry patch this summer. They're easy to grow and fresh berries taste terrific!

2-1/2 c. all-purpose flour	1-1/2 c. strawberries, sliced
2/3 c. plus 1-1/2 T. sugar, divided	1 c. non-fat buttermilk
1 t. baking soda	1/2 c. margarine, melted
3/4 t. cinnamon	1-1/4 t. vanilla extract
1/2 t. salt	1 egg, lightly beaten
	1 egg white, lightly beaten

Combine flour, 2/3 cup sugar, baking soda, cinnamon and salt in a large bowl; stir well. Add strawberries and mix. Make a well in the center of the mixture. Combine buttermilk, margarine, vanilla, egg, and egg white; blend well. Add to dry ingredients and stir until just moistened. Divide batter evenly among 18 muffin cups, coated with cooking spray. Sprinkle remaining sugar evenly over tops of muffins. Bake at 350 degrees for 25 minutes or until toothpick inserted in center comes out clean. Remove from pans immediately and let cool on a wire rack.

Jo Ann & Vickie started in 1984 with one telephone number for Gooseberry Patch which they rotated between each other's homes during "phone shifts." In those days, it was not uncommon for shoppers to hear dogs barking or kids laughing in the background while Vickie & Jo Ann took phone orders.

Chocolate Chip Puffins
Jo Ann

Make these pumpkin muffins a day or two ahead for the best flavor.
They're good for an after-school treat with an icy glass of milk.

1/2 c. sliced almonds
1-2/3 c. all-purpose flour
1 c. sugar
1 T. pumpkin pie spice
1 t. baking soda
1/4 t. baking powder

1/4 t. salt
2 eggs
1 c. pumpkin
1 stick butter, melted
1 c. chocolate chips

Place almonds on a baking sheet and bake at 350 degrees for 5 minutes or until lightly toasted. Remove from oven and let cool. Combine flour, sugar, pie spice, baking soda, baking powder and salt in a large bowl. Break eggs into a smaller bowl; add pumpkin and butter whisking until well blended. Stir in chocolate chips and cooled almonds. Pour into dry ingredients and mix until just moistened. Spoon batter into greased muffin cups. Bake at 350 degrees for 20 to 25 minutes or until the center springs back when lightly touched. Cool muffins on a wire rack.

"My dad began working for us in 1985. He would hand-write the names and addresses of everyone we shipped a package to in his special UPS book everyday. We have computers to keep track of those lists now, but I still have all of dad's old log books."

Vickie
1999

Italian Easter Bread

Barb Bargdill
Gooseberry Patch

Our family loves this bread served warm with butter.

1/2 c. warm water
2 pkgs. active dry yeast
1/2 c. milk, scalded
1/2 c. sugar
1 t. salt
2 eggs, beaten

1/2 c. shortening, softened
4-1/2 to 5 cups all-purpose flour
2 t. lemon extract
1/2 c. golden raisins
1 doz. white-shell eggs
1 pkg. egg coloring kit

Pour water into a large mixing bowl; add yeast and stir until dissolved. Cool milk to lukewarm and add yeast mixture. Add sugar, salt, eggs, shortening and lemon extract. Blend in flour and knead until dough is smooth and elastic, about 10 minutes; add raisins. shape dough in to a ball and place in an oiled bowl. Cover with a towel and let rest in a warm place until double in size, about 2 hours. Tint uncooked eggs according to dye package instructions; let dry while dough is rising. Divide dough into 3 portions. Roll each out into equal lengths and braid. Form braid into a circle and place on a greased cookie sheet. If desired, place eggs between each "nest" or braid, the eggs will cook while baking, cover and let rise 40 minutes. Bake at 350 degrees for 35 to 45 minutes.

Matt & Emily share breakfast with a new friend -1988

Apricot Crescents

Rene Smith
Shawnee, OK

Serve these with a steaming mug of chamomile tea and fresh fruit. Perfect for breakfast or a light brunch.

1 c. butter
2 c. all-purpose flour
1 egg yolk
1/2 c. sour cream

1/4 c. plus 2 T. sugar, divided
1/2 c. apricot preserves
1/2 c. shredded coconut
1/4 c. pecans, finely chopped

Cut butter into flour until mixture resembles coarse crumbs. Beat egg yolk with sour cream; add to crumb mixture and blend well. Divide into fourths and press into round shapes between layers of plastic wrap. Chill several hours or overnight. Sprinkle 2 tablespoons sugar on a flat surface and roll each portion of dough into a 10-inch circle. Turn dough circles over so sugared side is up. Combine preserves, coconut and pecans; spread over circles. Cut each circle into 12 pie-shaped wedges and roll into a crescent shape, beginning at the wide end. Sprinkle each rolled crescent with remaining sugar. Place one inch apart on an ungreased baking sheet. Bake at 350 degrees for 15 to 17 minutes or until lightly browned. Immediately remove from oven and place on wire racks to cool. Makes 4 dozen.

Jay and Shelby helped build two large packing tables for Gooseberry Patch shortly after Vickie & Jo Ann finished the second catalog in 1986. Both tables are still in use in the Gooseberry Patch warehouse today.

Pumpkin Bread

Ruth Naples
Mexico, ME

This is a good bread for bake sales and gift-giving.

3-1/3 c. all-purpose flour, sifted
2 t. baking soda
3 c. sugar
1 t. cinnamon
1 t. nutmeg

4 eggs, beaten
2 c. canned pumpkin
1 c. oil
2/3 c. cold water

Sift together flour, baking soda, sugar, cinnamon and nutmeg in a large bowl. Combine eggs, pumpkin, oil and water and blend into dry ingredients; mix until smooth. Divide batter into thirds, and pour into 9"x4" greased and floured loaf pans. Bake at 350 degrees for one hour or until centers are done. Cool slightly in pans then turn onto wire racks to finish cooling. Makes 3 loaves.

Dear Vickie & Jo Ann,

"My Gooseberry Patch books remind me of gentleness and good times and somehow always bring thoughts of my precious grandma. I used to think I had the privilege of having the most wonderful grandmother in the world, but your books tell me the world is filled with loving grandmothers. I shall try to be one myself."

Peggy Tully, Sulphur Springs, TX

Bread Basket

Noelle's Favorite Scones

Elizabeth Timmins
Gooseberry Patch Artisan

Just perfect with a cup of tea. There's nothing I like better than setting a table with pretty tea cups, a favorite tea pot, little tea sandwiches and sweets. To begin, I choose a theme, such as Sister's Tea, and invite sisters, as well as my sister. It's fun to think up different themes and then plan a menu to reflect the theme. I served these scones at a bridal tea party I had for my niece, Noelle.

2 c. all-purpose flour	1 T. baking powder
1 t. sugar	1 c. heavy cream
1 t. salt	

Sift together the dry ingredients in a large bowl. Add the cream, a little at a time, to form a soft ball. Knead gently and roll out to 1/2-inch thick. Cut with a round or shaped cookie cutter. Bake at 425 degrees on an ungreased baking sheet for 10 to 12 minutes, or until golden. Serve with Devonshire cream. Makes 8 to 10 scones.

Devonshire Cream:

8-oz. pkg. cream cheese, softened	1/2 c. sour cream
	2 T. powdered sugar

In a small bowl, beat the cream cheese until smooth. Add the sour cream and sugar and beat well. Refrigerate until ready to serve. Makes 1-1/3 cups.

Carrot Bread

Lou Ann Leonard
Blaine, MN

Handed down from my husband's grandmother, this is one recipe our family has made for years. Enjoying it now brings back many warm memories of times when all our grandparents were with us.

2 c. sugar
1-1/2 c. oil
4 eggs
3 c. all-purpose flour
2 t. baking powder

1 t. baking soda
1 t. salt
2 c. carrots, grated
1/2 c. nuts, chopped

Mix the sugar and oil together; add eggs, one at a time. Blend together flour, baking powder, baking soda, salt, carrots and nuts. Bake at 375 degrees for 45 minutes or until toothpick comes out clean after inserted in middle of bread. Makes 2 loaves.

Spice Glaze

Ann Magner
New Port Richey, FL

Drizzle on warm slices of bread or muffin tops.

1 t. cinnamon
1/4 c. milk
1 t. vanilla

1/2 t. nutmeg
1 c. powdered sugar

Blend all ingredients together until smooth adding additional milk or powdered sugar until mixture reaches desired consistency.

Bread Basket

Texas-Size Lemon Muffins

Traci Leigh Holt
Lake Jackson, TX

Baked in large muffin tins, these big lemon muffins are wonderful!
They're not only good for breakfast, they're great served
with chicken salad or fresh fruit.

1-3/4 c. all-purpose flour
3/4 t. baking soda
1 t. baking powder
1/4 t. salt
1-1/2 c. sugar, divided

4 T. lemon zest, divided
1 egg
8 oz. sour cream
1 lg. lemon, juiced and divided
1/4 c. butter, melted

Combine flour, baking soda, baking powder, salt and one cup sugar
in a large bowl, make a well in the center; set aside. Mix together 2
tablespoons lemon zest, egg, sour cream, half the lemon juice and
butter, add to the center of the dry mixture. Blend well and spoon into
large greased muffin pans. Bake at 350 degrees for 20 minutes. Blend
together remaining sugar, lemon juice and zest. Drizzle glaze over tops
of warm muffins. Makes 6 large muffins.

"Cowboy" Kyle rustles
up some fun at the zoo
-1995

Soft Pretzels

Tami Bowman
Gooseberry Patch

*Be adventurous! Instead of topping these with salt, try
your favorite dried herbs or hot pepper flakes.*

1 pkg. active dry yeast
1-1/2 c. lukewarm water
1 T. sugar
2 t. salt

4 c. all-purpose flour
1 egg yolk
1 T. water
1/4 c. coarse salt

Preheat oven to 425 degrees. Dissolve yeast in water. Add sugar and
salt; stir until dissolved. Add flour and mix well. Turn onto floured
board and knead for about 5 minutes. Divide dough into 16 equal
pieces. Roll into thin strips and shape into pretzels. Place on a
well-greased cookie sheet. Beat egg yolk with water; brush on pretzels.
Sprinkle with coarse salt and bake for 15 to 20 minutes.

*"We used to purchase some items
for our inventory just three at a
time. It was a 'big splurge' if we went
for six! Now we're buying quantities
in the thousands! It makes me
laugh now to think about how
hard we deliberated over stocking
six of one item!"*

Jo Ann
1999

Bread Basket

English Muffin Bread

Madge Bowman
Shreve, OH

The first time I made this bread we ate the whole loaf in one sitting!

2 pkgs. active dry yeast
1/2 c. warm water
5 c. all-purpose flour, divided
2 t. cinnamon
2 T. sugar
1 t. salt
1/4 t. baking soda

1-1/2 c. warm orange juice
1/4 c. vegetable oil
1/2 c. walnuts or pecans,
   chopped
1/2 c. dried apricots, chopped
yellow cornmeal

Dissolve yeast in water; set aside. Combine 2 cups flour, cinnamon, sugar, salt and baking soda; stir in yeast mixture. Blend in orange juice and oil. Beat mixture on low until thoroughly combined. Increase speed to high and blend for an additional 3 minutes. Stir in nuts, apricots and remaining flour to form a stiff batter. Do not knead. Spoon batter into 2 lightly oiled 9"x4" loaf pans; sprinkle yellow cornmeal over top of loaf. Cover and let rise for 45 minutes. Bake at 350 degrees for 35 to 40 minutes. Makes 2 loaves.

(1991)

Jo Ann & Vickie began sponsoring Gooseberry Patch contests in the catalog in 1991. The largest response...nearly 1,500 entries...came from the "Gooseberry Patch is My Favorite Country Catalog Because..." contest in 1994.

Caramel Rolls

Lisa Colombo
Appleton, WI

Growing up in a small village in Wisconsin, Grandma would send us to a nearby cheese factory for fresh cream and butter for these rolls.

1 c. brown sugar, packed
1 c. whipping cream
3-1/2 c. all-purpose flour, divided
3/4 c. sugar, divided
1 t. salt

1 pkg. active dry yeast
1 c. water
1/2 c. plus 2 T. butter, divided
1 egg
2 t. cinnamon

In an ungreased 13"x9" pan, combine brown sugar and whipping cream; set aside. In a large bowl, combine 1-1/2 cups flour, 1/4 cup sugar, salt and yeast; blend. In small saucepan, heat water and 2 tablespoons butter until very warm. Add warm liquid and egg to flour mixture. Blend at low speed until moistened. Beat at medium speed for 3 minutes. By hand, stir remaining flour to form a stiff dough. On floured surface, knead 2 to 3 minutes. Press or roll dough to form 15"x7" rectangle. In small bowl combine 1/2 cup sugar, cinnamon and remaining butter, spread over dough. Starting at long side, roll up tightly, seal edges. Cut into 15 rolls. Place rolls, cut side down, on top of brown sugar mixture Cover, let rise in warm place until light and double in size, 35 to 45 minutes. Bake at 400 degrees for 20 to 25 minutes or until lightly golden.

Dear Vickie & Jo Ann,

"Your books have evoked many wonderful childhood memories. My family was far from wealthy in the sense of money or material things, but we certainly felt the wealthiest in terms of love and fun!"

Shirley Young, Jersey Shore, PA

Bread Basket

Raisin Loaf

Karen Stoner
Gooseberry Patch

I've had this recipe at least 25 years, it's great!

3/4 c. sugar
1/4 c. butter, softened
1 egg
1 T. orange zest
2 c. all-purpose flour
1-/2 t. salt

2 t. baking powder
1/2 t. baking soda
1 c. milk
1 c. raisins
1/2 c. walnuts, chopped

Beat together sugar, butter, egg and orange zest until creamy. In a separate bowl, combine dry ingredients; stir into creamed mixture alternately with milk. Mix raisins and nuts into last portion of dry ingredients before adding to batter. Pour into a greased 9"x4" loaf pan. Bake at 350 degrees for 55 minutes or until center is done. Let bread cool in pan for 10 minutes, remove from pan and allow to cool completely on wire rack. Makes one loaf.

Jo Ann enjoys spending an occasional afternoon in the kitchen "inventing" new recipes. She loves to whip up fresh-baked breads, pasta dishes and any recipe to which she can add the word "surprise"!

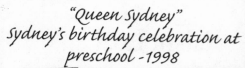
"Queen Sydney"
Sydney's birthday celebration at preschool -1998

Emily, Matt & Vickie with Matt's 1st car -1995

Vickie & Emily enjoying a day at Lake Erie -1990

Robbie & Jo Ann celebrate Jo Ann's birthday! -1995

Family Dinners

Remember those Sunday dinners? Jo Ann with her brother, sister & cousins.

Homestyle Swiss Steak

Diane Long
Gooseberry Patch

This is an old family recipe we always serve with mashed potatoes.

1/4 c. all-purpose flour
1 t. salt
1/4 t. pepper
1-1/2 to 2 lbs. round steak

4 T. margarine
1 to 2 onions, chopped
12-oz. can vegetable cocktail
  juice

Combine flour, salt and pepper and spread half on a wooden cutting board. Place steak on board, sprinkle remaining flour mixture on top and pound beef with a mallet. Add margarine to a large saucepan and sauté with meat; browning meat well on both sides. Stir onions and vegetable juice into saucepan; cover and simmer for one hour.

Shelby, Vickie, Emily & Matt pose for a springtime family photo -1990

Stuffed Ham Rolls

Cathy Elgin
St. Louis Park, MN

A great dish served with sauerkraut or fresh corn on the cob.

1/4 c. onion, chopped
1/4 c. celery, finely chopped
1/4 c. butter
2 T. parsley
1/2 t. poultry seasoning
1/2 t. pepper
1-1/2 c. soda crackers, crushed

1 egg, beaten
1/2 c. water
1-1/2 c. turkey or chicken,
    cooked and diced
3 c. Cheddar cheese, diced
20 slices of ham

Mix all ingredients, except ham slices, in a large bowl. Place
2 tablespoons of filling into center of each slice of ham; then roll.
Place seam side down on cookie sheet and cover with foil. Bake at
350 degrees for 20 minutes.

Savory Beef

Kristi Warzocha
Lakewood, OH

A favorite recipe from an old 1930's church cookbook.

3 lg. onions, sliced
3 T. shortening
2-lb. round roast, sliced
3 T. all-purpose flour

1/4 t. cloves
1 pt. beef broth
2 T. vinegar
1 t. catsup

In a Dutch oven, cook onions in shortening until onions are tender.
Add beef slices and brown. Combine flour and cloves, sprinkle over
beef. Stir in broth, vinegar and catsup and simmer, covered, for
1-1/2 to 2 hours. Serves 6.

Crispy Chicken

Mia Lokensgard
Aurora, IL

This recipe originated in Hawaii...it's easy to make and so delicious!

1/2 c. soy sauce
1/2 c. sugar
1 slice ginger, crushed
1 clove garlic, crushed
2 T. wine

1/2 t. salt
3-lb. chicken, cubed
1 c. corn flake cereal crumbs
1/4 c. sesame seeds

In large bowl, combine soy sauce, sugar, ginger, garlic, wine and salt. Marinate chicken pieces for approximately one hour. Roll chicken in cereal crumbs and sesame seeds. Line a shallow baking pan with foil and add chicken, skin side up. Bake at 350 degrees for 30 to 45 minutes. Makes 4 to 6 servings.

Honey Roasted Pork

Sultana Purpora
Englewood, OH

Yummy served with homemade stuffing and roasted potatoes!

2 to 3-lb. boneless pork loin
  roast
1/4 c. honey
2 T. Dijon mustard

2 T. mixed or black peppercorns,
  crushed
1/2 t. dried thyme, crushed
1/2 t. salt

Place roast on a lightly greased rack in a shallow roasting pan. Combine honey and remaining ingredients; brush about half of mixture over roast. Bake at 325 degrees for one hour; brush with remaining honey mixture. Bake 30 additional minutes or until meat thermometer inserted in the thickest portion registers 160 degrees.

Family Dinners

Dutch Meat Loaf

Gwen Stutler
Emporia, KS

Growing up, I remember this recipe was requested many times by my dad and brother. Even now that we've moved away from home, this recipe is popular when the family gets together.

1-1/2 lbs. ground beef
1 c. soft bread crumbs
1 sm. onion, finely chopped
1/3 c. green pepper, finely chopped
2 eggs, beaten

1-1/2 t. salt
1/4 t. pepper
1 c. tomato sauce, divided
1 T. brown sugar
1 T. vinegar
1-1/2 t. mustard

Combine beef, bread crumbs, onion, green pepper, eggs, salt, pepper and 1/2 cup of tomato sauce; press into an 8-1/2"x4-1/2" loaf pan. Bake at 350 degrees for one hour. Combine remaining 1/2 cup of tomato sauce, brown sugar, vinegar and mustard in a small saucepan; cook over medium heat until thoroughly heated. Transfer loaf to a platter and spoon sauce over meat loaf. Makes 6 to 8 servings.

Dear Vickie & Jo Ann,

"Reading a Gooseberry Patch book is like going through a candy store...you can take what you like and enjoy it! I'm partial to the simple heirloom traditions that people have in their families and I like to adapt some of them to my own family."

Mel Wolk, St. Peters, MO

Pork Chops & Stuffing

Barbara Schmeckpeper
Elwood, IL

I've been making this recipe for 28 years and it's still one of my favorites! The mandarin oranges and brown sugar make it special.

6 pork chops
1 T. shortening
2 t. salt, divided
1 c. celery, chopped
3/4 c. onion, chopped
1/4 c. butter, melted
1/4 c. brown sugar, packed

5 c. bread, cubed
1 egg, beaten
1 t. dried sage
1/2 t. dried thyme
1/8 t. pepper
11-oz. can mandarin oranges, drained

Brown pork chops in shortening; remove to a platter and season with one teaspoon salt. Brown celery and onion lightly in melted butter; stir in brown sugar. Combine bread cubes with egg and seasonings and add to browned vegetables. Stir in oranges and gently mix. Spoon stuffing into the center of a 10" baking dish. Place pork chops around the stuffing and cover with foil. Bake at 325 degrees for one hour and 15 minutes. Makes 6 servings.

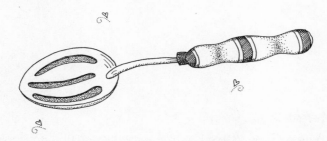

"Vickie and I want to feel proud of everything we offer. We want to make sure our packages look like gifts when they arrive, not just another box in the mail. From lining the top of the package with a piece of our very own tissue paper to the way the box smells so good when you open it...it's the special details we care about."

Jo Ann
1998

Chicken Pot Pie

Dana Stewart
Gooseberry Patch Artisan

This is one of my "old reliable" recipes that serves us well when we invite friends to dinner and aren't sure what they like...or don't like!

1/2 c. onion, chopped
2 celery stalks, chopped
1/2 c. mushrooms, sliced
1/4 c. butter
1/3 c. all-purpose flour
1 t. dried thyme
salt and pepper to taste

2 c. chicken broth
3/4 c. milk
2 med. potatoes, diced
3 carrots, peeled and chopped
1/2 c. frozen peas
1/2 c. frozen corn
2 c. chicken, cooked and cubed

In a medium saucepan, sauté onion, celery and mushrooms in butter. Stir in flour, thyme, salt and pepper. Add broth and milk. Cook over medium heat until thick and bubbly; set aside. Microwave potatoes, carrots, peas and corn until crisp-tender; drain any water. Add vegetables to onion mixture, cook until bubbly; add chicken. Pour into a 2-quart casserole dish and top with pastry.

Pie Crust:

1-1/4 c. all-purpose flour
1/4 t. salt

1/3 c. shortening
3 to 4 T. cold water

Stir together flour and salt. Using a pastry blender, cut in shortening until mixture is the size of peas. Sprinkle one to 2 tablespoon cold water in; gently toss with a fork. Repeat, using one tablespoon of water at a time until the pastry is moistened. Roll in a 10-inch circle. Lay pastry over chicken mixture in casserole dish; flute edges. Cut slits to vent, or use mini-cookie cutters to cut out shapes in pastry. Bake at 450 degrees for 15 to 20 minutes.

Chili Relleno Casserole

JoAnn Bradley
Blythe, CA

This was always my mother's favorite recipe and one I made sure to serve when she visited.

2 4-oz. cans whole green chili peppers, seeded
1 c. Monterey Jack cheese, grated

1 c. Cheddar cheese, grated
1 doz. eggs, beaten
1 c. milk
salt and pepper to taste

Heat oven to 350 degrees. Coat a 13"x9" pan with non-stick cooking spray. Cover bottom of pan with a layer of open chili peppers. Cover peppers with Monterey Jack cheese. Place another layer of peppers on cheese. Cover this layer of peppers with Cheddar cheese. Mix eggs, milk, salt and pepper. Pour egg mixture over layer of peppers and cheese. Place in oven for 45 minutes. Take out of oven when golden brown on top and a knife comes out clean when sliced in the middle. Let sit for 5 minutes before cutting. Serve with salsa and corn chips.

Fresh Tomato Salsa:

3 tomatoes, chopped
1/2 c. onion, chopped
2 cloves garlic, minced
1/2 c. fresh cilantro, chopped

2-oz.can. chopped green chilies
1/8 t. sugar
1/4 c. water

Combine all ingredients, mixing well. Refrigerate until ready to serve.

While Gooseberry Patch has grown since the early days, Vickie & Jo Ann still love to answer phone orders, wrap packages and write letters to their "Gooseberry friends!"

Mexican Stuffed Shells

Julie Wise
Delaware, OH

Stuff the shells with Italian sausage and hot picante sauce for a spicier taste. We serve it with a crunchy salad and warm bread.

12-oz. jar picante sauce
15-oz. can tomato sauce
1/2 c. water
1 lb. ground beef, browned
4-oz. can chopped green chilies
2 c. Cheddar or Co-Jack cheese,
   shredded and divided

2.8-oz. can French-fried onions,
   divided
12 lg. pasta shells, cooked and
   drained

In small bowl, mix picante sauce, tomato sauce and water. Stir half of the sauce into the ground beef. Add chilies, one cup cheese and half of the onions; mix well. Spread half of the remaining sauce on bottom of 13"x9" pan. Stuff cooked shells with meat mixture. Arrange shells in pan and top with sauce. Cover and bake for 30 minutes. Top with remaining onions and cheese. Bake uncovered 5 minutes.

Smile! Vickie's birthday at her favorite Mexican restaurant! -1998

Stromboli

Tina Troudt
Cheyenne, WY

This is a recipe we've come to really enjoy. My husband says he loves it even more than pizza!

1 loaf frozen French Bread
   dough
14-oz. can pizza sauce
1/4 lb. ham, thinly sliced
1/4 lb. hard salami, sliced
1 t. dried basil, divided

1 t. dried oregano, divided
3 oz. Provolone cheese, thinly
   sliced
1 c. mozzarella cheese, shredded
cornmeal

Unroll dough and lay flat on greased cookie sheet. Spread pizza sauce along one half of dough lengthwise. Arrange ham slices lengthwise down the same side of the dough. Place salami on top. Sprinkle with 1/2 teaspoon basil and 1/2 teaspoon oregano. Arrange Provolone cheese on top and cover with mozzarella cheese. Sprinkle with remaining basil and oregano. Bring edges of dough together, securely seal ends. Sprinkle with cornmeal and carefully turn over. Sprinkle cornmeal on other side. Bake at 375 degrees for 20 to 22 minutes.

1985

In the early years, Vickie & Jo Ann organized catalog mailings from Vickie's dining room. Vickie would spread the catalogs out across the room according to zip code until she could no longer see the floor! Jo Ann would then bundle the catalogs together and take them to the post office in town.

Family Dinners

Biscuit-Topped Beef

Cathy Elgin
St. Louis Park, MN

I've served this many times; there are never any leftovers! This is also great served over cooked noodles; just eliminate the biscuit topping.

1-1/2 lbs. ground beef
2 T. dried minced onion
1 to 2 T. dried parsley flakes
1/4 t. garlic powder
1 t. salt

1/4 to 1/2 t. pepper
7-oz. can mushrooms, drained
10-1/2 oz. can vegetable soup
1 c. sour cream
1/2 c. milk

Brown beef with onion, parsley and garlic. Stir in salt, pepper, mushrooms and soup; simmer 15 minutes. Blend in sour cream and milk. Heat thoroughly, but do not boil. Place in a 9"x9" baking dish; set aside while preparing biscuit topping.

Biscuit Topping:

1-1/2 c. all-purpose flour
2 t. baking powder
1 t. paprika
1/2 t. salt
1/2 t. celery seed

1/4 t. white pepper
1/4 c. shortening
3/4 c. milk
1 t. poppy seeds

Sift flour, baking powder, paprika, salt, celery seed and pepper into mixing bowl. Cut in shortening; add milk. Stir until mixture is just moistened. Drop by tablespoonfuls onto stroganoff; sprinkle with poppy seeds. Bake at 400 degrees for 20 to 25 minutes. Serves 6 to 8.

"We love reading letters from our Gooseberry Patch friends. It warms our hearts to know we've been such a special part of your homes and families for the past 15 years."

Jo Ann
1999

Bacon & Mushroom Pasta

Deberah Green
Gooseberry Patch

*When you're on the go, just add a salad and rolls
for a quick and delicious meal.*

1 lb. shell pasta
3 bacon slices, crisply cooked
   and crumbled
8-oz. can mushrooms
1 to 2 T. butter

2 t. sugar
1 c. chicken broth
2 T. fresh parsley, chopped
2 c. mozzarella cheese, shredded
1/4 c. grated Parmesan cheese

Prepare pasta according to package directions. Mix next 6 ingredients together and place in a 13"x9" casserole dish. Sprinkle with cheeses and bake at 350 degrees for 40 minutes.

Noodle & Rice Casserole

Becky Sykes
Gooseberry Patch

*This casserole is a favorite in our family. It's also great to take
to a Gooseberry Patch potluck because it feeds so many!*

1 c. butter
1/2 lb. thin noodles, uncooked
2 c. instant rice, uncooked
2 10-3/4 oz. cans French onion
   soup

2 8-oz. cans chicken broth
1 t. soy sauce
1 c. water
8-oz. can sliced water chestnuts,
   drained

Melt butter in a large saucepan; add noodles. Cook over medium heat until until lightly browned; stir frequently. Add rice and remaining ingredients; mix well. Turn into a 3-quart casserole and bake uncovered at 350 degrees for 45 minutes. Serves 12 to 14.

Teriyaki Chicken

Tracy Onoz
Gooseberry Patch Artisan

I made this recipe for a man several years ago, to fool him into thinking I was an excellent cook...it worked! He married me, and now, two beautiful children later, he does most of the cooking!

1/2 c. all-purpose flour
1/2 t. salt
1/8 t. pepper
2 lbs. chicken breast, cut into
  strips
2 eggs, beaten

oil
1/3 c. soy sauce
1/3 c. honey
1 T. dry sherry
1 clove garlic, minced
1 t. fresh ginger, grated

Combine flour, salt and pepper. Dip chicken strips in eggs, then coat with flour mixture. Pour enough oil in a large saucepan to equal 1/2 inch; turn heat to medium-high. When oil is hot, add chicken strips and cook until golden brown. In a separate small saucepan, heat soy sauce, honey, sherry, garlic and ginger. When chicken strips have been removed from saucepan, drain and dip into honey mixture; place on a baking sheet. Bake strips at 250 degrees for 20 minutes; brush with remaining honey mixture after 10 minutes.

Surf Side Fettuccini

Terri Lloyd
Florence, MT

This is fantastic hot or served cold the next day!

12-oz. pkg. fettuccini
1 c. salad shrimp, cooked
1 c. imitation crab, cubed
1 c. frozen broccoli
1 c. carrots, thinly sliced

1/4 c. butter or margarine
1 clove garlic, chopped
Garnish: fresh Parmesan cheese,
  grated

Cook fettuccini according to package directions. While the fettuccini is boiling, sauté the remaining ingredients together until the carrots are crisp-tender and the water from the broccoli has evaporated. Toss mixture with drained fettuccini noodles and sprinkle with the freshly grated Parmesan cheese.

Kyle's headed to the sandbox for a day of fun in the sun! - 1989

Beef Stroganoff

Grandma Tootsie
Jo Ann's mom

Leftovers of this family recipe are even terrific! Sometimes I add a dash of red wine and garlic for extra flavor, then I'll let it simmer for hours so the flavors can blend.

1 lb. beef tenderloin
3 T. all-purpose flour
1/4 c. butter
1 onion, chopped
1/2 lb. mushrooms

1/4 t. Worcestershire sauce
1 c. sour cream
1 t. salt
1 t. pepper

Coat beef with flour; cut into 1/4-inch strips. Heat butter in a heavy saucepan and add beef; brown on all sides. Remove meat; set aside. Add onion and mushrooms to the saucepan, cook over low heat for 5 minutes. Return meat to saucepan and stir in remaining ingredients; heat to boiling. Serve over homemade noodles. Serves 4.

Homemade Noodles:

3 egg yolks, beaten
1 egg, beaten
1 T. salt

3 T. cold water
2 c. all-purpose flour

Combine egg yolks and egg; blend in salt and cold water. Work flour into mixture to make a stiff dough; divide into 3 equal parts. On a lightly floured surface roll out one portion of dough as thin as possible. Let rest 10 minutes; repeat with remaining 2 portions of dough. Lightly dust one section of dough with flour, roll up jelly-roll style. Cut across the roll into 1/4-inch wide strips; repeat with remaining dough. Separate noodles and let dry 10 minutes. Drop noodles into a stockpot of boiling water. Boil until tender, 5 to 10 minutes. Remove from water and keep warm until ready to top with stroganoff.

Cape Cod Turkey Delight

Martha Dennis
Swartz Creek, MI

Served with cottage cheese sprinkled with pecans, I think this makes such a nice luncheon for the neighbor ladies.

2/3 c. fat-free mayonnaise-type
   salad dressing
loaf of bread, sliced

1 lb. turkey, sliced
16-oz. can cranberry sauce
1/2 lb. Cheddar cheese, sliced

Prepare by using a light coating of mayonnaise-type salad dressing on bread. Add turkey slice. Then place a thin layer of cranberry sauce under the turkey and a slice of Cheddar cheese on top. Add additional slice of bread. Microwave on medium for 10 seconds. Serves 6.

French Dip Sandwich

Katie Sullivan
Westerville, OH

A favorite sandwich served on sourdough bread or crusty rolls.

5-lb. boneless rump roast
1 T. garlic powder
1/2 t. seasoned salt
1/4 t. cayenne pepper
1/2 t. dried oregano

1/2 t. dried rosemary
2 beef bouillon cubes
1 onion, finely chopped
2 10-1/2 oz. cans beef broth

Place ingredients in a slow cooker on low for 8 to 10 hours, or turn temperature to high for 4 to 6 hours. Thinly slice meat and reserve broth for dipping. Serves 6 to 8.

Italian Casserole

Gail Banasiak
Dayton, OH

*Perfect for a family get-together. Not only is this
casserole really good, it serves a crowd!*

16-oz. pkg. noodles
1-1/2 lbs. bulk Italian sausage
1-1/2 lbs. ground beef
1 c. onion, chopped
1 c. green pepper, chopped
2 15-oz. cans tomato sauce
2 6-oz. cans tomato paste
1/2 c. water

1 t. dried basil
1 t. dried oregano
1/4 t. garlic powder
15-oz. can corn, drained
6-oz. can sliced ripe olives,
  drained
8-oz. Cheddar cheese, shredded

Cook noodles according to package directions; set aside. In a Dutch
oven, cook sausage, ground beef, onion and pepper until meat is
thoroughly browned and vegetables are tender. Drain fat. Add tomato
sauce, tomato paste, water, basil, oregano and garlic powder. Simmer
for 15 minutes. Stir in corn and olives; simmer 5 minutes longer. Stir
noodles in sausage mixture; mixing well. Divide equally into 2 lightly
oiled 13"x9" baking dishes; top with cheese. Bake at 350 degrees for
25 to 30 minutes. Serves 16 to 20.

(1985)

The very first Gooseberry Patch logo,
designed by Jo Ann & Vickie in
early 1985, featured three geese
dressed up in red-checked
kerchiefs and bows. The logo
has changed over time, but a
hand-painted version of the original
still greets visitors near the front
door of Gooseberry Patch.

Hot Chicken Salad

Kris Lammers
Gooseberry Patch Artisan

Always a hit at potlucks, I've been making this for years. Recently, while watching me make it, my kids discovered there are onions in it. They've always liked it, but never knew about the onions!

1 lg. bunch celery, chopped
1/2 c. onion, finely chopped
1-1/2 c. chicken, cooked and
   chopped
8-oz. can sliced water chestnuts,
   drained

1 c. mayonnaise
2 c. Cheddar cheese, shredded
1-1/2 c. potato chips, crushed
1/2 c. slivered almonds

In a large mixing bowl, combine celery, onion, chicken, water chestnuts and mayonnaise; mixing well. Place in a 2-quart baking dish; layer in order cheese, potato chips and almonds. Bake at 400 degrees for 20 minutes, or until heated through and golden on top.

Vickie & Jo Ann sprinkled the pages
of the Autumn 1990 catalog with
answers to some of the "most asked"
questions from their customers.
Here's how Vickie described spending her
leisure time: "What leisure time?
Kids keep me busy running...soccer,
gymnastics, baton, jazz and baseball!
I love decorating my home, antiquing,
traveling around New England
& curling up on the couch at the
end of the day."

Family Dinners

Spinach Pie

Nancy Burton
Wamego, KS

This is a terrific, light meal I like to serve with muffins and fresh fruit. It's nice for brunch or a special occasion.

3 eggs, lightly beaten
1 lb. cottage cheese
10-oz. pkg. frozen spinach,
    thawed and drained

8 oz. Cheddar cheese, shredded
1/4 c. butter, melted
3 T. all-purpose flour
salt blend to taste

Combine all ingredients. Pour into a 9" pie plate. Bake at 325 degrees for one hour. Cool slightly and cut into wedges.

Country-Style Ribs

Joanne West
Beavercreek, OH

Maple syrup makes ordinary ribs really special!

3 lbs. country-style ribs
1 c. maple syrup
1/2 c. applesauce
1/4 c. catsup

3 T. lemon juice
1/4 t. paprika
1/4 t. garlic powder
1/4 t. cinnamon

Place ribs in a Dutch oven; cover with water. Bring to a boil, reduce heat and simmer 10 minutes. Place ribs in an oiled 13"x9" baking dish. Combine remaining ingredients and pour over ribs. Bake at 325 degrees one to 2 hours, or until meat is tender. Serves 4.

Before starting Gooseberry Patch, Vickie worked as a legal secretary and a flight attendant. Jo Ann was a first-grade teacher at a local elementary school.

Chicken Tetrazzini

Grandma Tootsie
Jo Ann's mom

This family favorite is one of my special dishes.

2 frying chickens
1 lb. thin spaghetti, uncooked
1 stick butter
1 green pepper, chopped
1 lg. onion, chopped
1 clove garlic, minced
5 T. all-purpose flour
2 c. warm milk
2 10-oz. cans mushroom soup
1/2 c. pimento, minced

1/2 t. pepper
1/2 c. dry sherry
1 T. Worcestershire sauce
1 c. celery, chopped
4-oz. can sliced mushrooms
4 c. Cheddar cheese, grated and
   divided
1/2 c. fresh Parmesan cheese,
   grated
1 c. slivered almonds, divided

Boil chicken until juices run clear when pierced with a fork. Cool and bone; reserve stock. Cook spaghetti in chicken stock according to package directions. Drain and divide equally between 2 13"x9" baking dishes; set aside. Sauté green pepper, onion and garlic in butter; add flour. Stir in milk and soup; stir until smooth. Add pimento, pepper, sherry, Worcestershire, celery, mushrooms, 3 cups cheese, Parmesan cheese and 1/2 cup almonds. Simmer 5 minutes. Spoon over spaghetti, top with remaining cheese and almonds. Bake at 350 degrees for 15 minutes. Serves 18.

Dear Vickie & Jo Ann,

"My daughter, granddaughter and I look forward to each and every one of your books. They have given us a great deal of pleasure and some wonderful times together working on projects, gifts and just good food!"

Sharon Taylor, Mansfield Depot, CT

Summertime Chicken

Tamara Wallace
Roscoe, IL

Quick and juicy, this dish is great for a warm weather gathering of friends and family. Serve with a side of fresh garden vegetables.

1-1/2 c. vegetable broth
2 T. Worcestershire sauce
1-1/2 t. hot pepper sauce
1 t. cayenne pepper

1 t. pepper
2-1/2 lbs. skinless chicken breasts

Combine broth and seasonings in a shallow baking dish. Mix well. Add chicken breasts, cover and refrigerate for one hour. Lightly spray frying pan with non-stick spray and add chicken breasts with one-half of the marinade. Simmer 30 minutes, or until juices run clear. Makes 6 servings.

Robbie, Jo Ann, Sydney & Jay enjoying a neighborhood 4th of July party - 1998

Apple Cider Turkey

Cindy Watts
Conyers, GA

This is a spicy, delicious change to the usual roast turkey.

5 to 7-lb. turkey breast
1 c. apple cider vinegar
1/4 c. salt

1/4 c. pepper
1/4 c. oil
2 T. dried parsley

Place turkey breast in a large oven roasting bag. Combine apple cider vinegar, salt, pepper, oil and parsley in a container with a tight fitting lid and shake until mixed thoroughly. Pour over turkey and bake at 300 degrees for 2-1/2 to 3-1/2 hours, or until done.

*"With the college soccer season falling right
in the middle of their holiday break, many of Jay's
players spend Thanksgiving day with us. This year we had 20 hungry
college soccer players crowd around our dining room table for dinner. It
was like having lots of extra sons!"*

Jo Ann
1998

Chicken-Artichoke Ring

Joy Stephens
Orange, CA

This is a recipe that's just perfect for a bridal shower, baby shower or anytime you're planning a special get-together with friends.

4 skinless chicken breasts, cooked and chopped
6-oz. jar marinated artichoke hearts, chopped
12 oz. fontina cheese
1 c. fresh Parmesan cheese, grated
1 lg. onion, chopped
5 green onions, chopped

1-1/2 t. dried thyme
1 T. fresh parsley, chopped
6 eggs
1/2 c. heavy cream
salt and pepper to taste
1/2 c. plus 2 T. unsalted butter, melted
8-oz. pkg. phyllo dough

In a large bowl, combine chicken, artichoke hearts, cheeses, onions, thyme and parsley; mix well. In a separate bowl, blend together eggs and cream; add salt and pepper to taste. Add to chicken mixture; set aside. Brush 1/4 cup butter on the bottom and sides of a 10-inch Bundt® pan. Cut a sheet of phyllo dough in half. Line the pan with dough by pressing the sheet inside the pan. Each new sheet should overlap the previous one and the edges should drape over the side. Repeat with 3 sheets to cover the bottom of the Bundt® pan. Brush 1/4 cup melted butter over phyllo; top with chicken mixture. One edge at a time, bring overlapping dough on top of the chicken mixture to cover. Brush top of dough with 2 tablespoons butter. Bake at 350 degrees for one hour, or until dough is golden. Cool in the pan for 15 minutes. Remove from pan and cut into wedges.

Nearly 40 percent of all the products in our catalog are designed exclusively for Gooseberry Patch!

Grilled Pork Roast

Judy Kelly
St. Charles, MO

This is great served with roasted onion sauce!

5-lb. rolled boneless pork roast
1/4 c. olive oil

2 cloves garlic, minced
seasoned salt and pepper

Rub pork roast with oil, making sure to cover it well. Rub with garlic and season with salt and pepper. Cook on grill over indirect heat. Begin cooking when the coals are the hottest. Add another 6 to 7 charcoal briquettes to each side after one hour. Roast should be done in 2 hours; however test with a meat thermometer to be sure internal temperature is 160 degrees.

Roasted Onion Sauce:

1 med. sweet onion, quartered
1 t. olive oil
salt to taste

2/3 c. beef broth
1 t. soy sauce
4 t. pepper

Preheat oven to 350 degrees. Place onion wedges in a baking dish. Drizzle with the olive oil and sprinkle with salt. Stir to coat all of the pieces evenly. Roast onions, uncovered, until browned and soft, about one hour. Remove and let stand until slightly cooled. Place onions in a blender. Add broth and soy sauce, blend to a smooth purée. Transfer the sauce to a small saucepan; cover and set aside. Heat just before serving, adding pepper while heating.

Dear Vickie & Jo Ann,

"I feel like we're friends! Your catalog, a hot cup of tea and a warm fire...heaven!"

Patti Strain, Terra Haute, IN

Sweet & Sour Pork

Ann Magner
New Port Richey, FL

You can enjoy this tasty recipe at home; it's so easy
and takes very little time to prepare.

1-1/2 lbs. cooked pork
3/4 c. plus 1 T. soy sauce,
   divided
3 T. oil
3 green peppers, cut into strips
1 onion, sliced

1 lb. 4-oz. can pineapple tidbits,
   drained and juice reserved
3 T. cornstarch
3 T. vinegar
1/3 c. sugar

Slice pork into strips and place in a shallow baking dish. Cover with 3/4 cup soy sauce and let stand for one hour. Turn meat several times to thoroughly marinate. Heat oil in a saucepan and sauté peppers and onion over high heat for one minute. Remove peppers and onion from saucepan; set aside. Add pork to skillet with juice from pineapple and bring to a boil. Reduce heat and simmer for 5 minutes. Add pineapple to peppers and onions stir to thoroughly mix and simmer one minute. Combine cornstarch, vinegar, sugar and one tablespoon soy sauce in a medium bowl, whisking until smooth and well blended. Pour into pork mixture and simmer until sauce thickens. Spoon over prepared white rice. Serves 4.

Dear Vickie & Jo Ann,

"The memories our 'Gooseberry Family' share with each other are something I can't describe...perhaps it is a sense of hope that we can return to times of a more caring, thoughtful, and slower-paced way of life."

Jenny Atkinson
Birmingham, AL

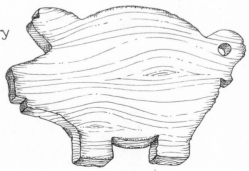

Autumn Hayride Casserole

Helen Murray
Piketon, OH

An easy to make-and-take casserole!

1 lb. ground beef, browned
1-1/2 t. salt, divided
1/2 t. chili powder
2 c. Cheddar cheese, shredded
    and divided
1/2 c. barbecue sauce
1-1/2 c. Mexican-style corn
8-oz. can tomato sauce

1 c. all-purpose flour
1/2 c. cornmeal
2 T. sugar
1 t. baking powder
1/4 c. butter
1/2 c. milk
1 egg, beaten

Combine ground beef, 1/2 teaspoon salt, chili powder, one cup Cheddar cheese, barbecue sauce, corn and tomato sauce; set aside. Combine flour, cornmeal, sugar, baking powder and one teaspoon salt, 1/2 cup cheese; cut in butter. Blend in milk and egg. Spread flour mixture over the bottom and sides of an ungreased 9" square baking pan. Pour ground beef mixture on top of crust. Bake at 400 degrees for 20 minutes; sprinkle with remaining cheese. Bake for an additional 3 to 5 minutes. Serves 6 to 8.

Jo Ann, Kyle & Ryan take a hayride to a nearby pumpkin farm -1990

Hearty Salisbury Steak

Sandy Dodson
Indianapolis, IN

Whenever I make this dish, I have fond memories of my Grandmother Katie. She always made sure everyone had enough to eat, no matter if it did stretch her pocketbook.

2 lbs. ground chuck
1 c. onion, chopped
1/2 c. bread crumbs
1 egg, beaten
1/4 c. green pepper, chopped
1 T. oil
2 T. all-purpose flour

1/2 t. salt
pepper to taste
2 c. water
1/2 t. browning sauce
8 new potatoes
1 c. baby carrots, peeled
1/2 c. pearl onions

Combine ground chuck, onion, bread crumbs, egg and green pepper in a large mixing bowl. Shape into 1/4-inch thick oval patties. Add oil to a deep skillet, sauté until thoroughly cooked. Drain drippings, leaving 2 tablespoons in the skillet. Add flour, salt and pepper to skillet, slowly add water. Continue to stir until broth begins to thicken, add browning sauce. Return patties to skillet, add potatoes, carrots and onions. Simmer one hour or until vegetables are tender. If the broth thickens too much while simmering, add more water as needed. Serves 6 to 8.

Dear Vickie & Jo Ann,

"I have been receiving your catalog for over 10 years now. I must say it has been a pleasure to watch your company grow, but even more so, to see your children grow up. Thank you for sharing photos with us, your fans. I always look for the family pictures first when I bring my catalog in from the mail!"

Jackie Hardy, Chickamauga, GA

Key Lime Grilled Chicken

Robin Stansberry
Talbott, TN

You can also use this for a great stir-fry sauce.

3 T. soy sauce
1 T. honey
1 T. olive oil
1 med. lime, juiced

3 cloves garlic, minced
4 boneless, skinless chicken
  breasts

Mix soy sauce, honey, olive oil, lime juice and garlic in a small bowl.
Arrange chicken in a baking dish and pour marinade over top.
Refrigerate one hour. Remove chicken from marinade; discard
marinade. Grill chicken over medium hot coals for 10 minutes
each side.

Tangy Ham Steak

Terri Demidovich
Charleston, SC

Easy to prepare, it's great when company's coming.

1/3 c. spicy brown mustard
1/4 c. honey

1/2 t. orange zest
2 lbs. ham steaks

Combine mustard, honey and zest. Brush over one side of ham steaks.
Grill over medium heat for 8 minutes; turn. Brush with honey mixture,
cook an additional 8 minutes or until heated through. Serves 6.

──── (1999) ────

Vickie & Jo Ann have been friends for more than 15 years now. Every
once in a while, they'll jump in the car for "girls day out" trips to flea
markets, antique stores or wherever the road takes them!

Spaghetti Casserole

Laura Strausberger
Cary, IL

One summer, my friend Chris and I planned a 4th of July family getaway. Unfortunately on the way, our van broke down and we had to be towed back to Las Vegas, 3-1/2 hours away! Once safely home, Chris invited us over to enjoy a casserole she'd made. It was wonderful, and tasted even better after all we'd been through!

1 c. onions, chopped
1 c. green pepper, chopped
1 T. butter
28-oz. can tomatoes, undrained
4-oz. can mushrooms, drained
3.8-oz. can sliced black olives, drained
2 t. dried oregano
1 lb. ground beef, browned and drained

12 oz. spaghetti, cooked and drained
2 c. Cheddar cheese, shredded
10-3/4 oz. can condensed cream of mushroom soup
1/4 c. water
1/4 c. Parmesan cheese, grated

In a large skillet, sauté onion and green pepper in butter until tender. Add tomatoes, mushrooms, olives and oregano. Add ground beef and simmer, uncovered, for 10 minutes. Place half of the spaghetti in a greased 13"x9" baking dish. Top with half of the vegetable mixture. Sprinkle with one cup of Cheddar cheese. Repeat layers. Mix soup and water until smooth; pour over casserole; sprinkle with Parmesan cheese. Bake, uncovered, at 350 degrees for 30 to 35 minutes or until heated through. Makes 12 servings.

Spinach Tortellini

Cathy Karnes
Manhattan Beach, CA

If you'd like to cut calories, use low-fat ingredients. They work just as well and you'll have a very healthy dish.

5 T. butter, melted
5 T. all-purpose flour
3 c. warm milk
1 c. fresh Parmesan cheese, grated

2 12-oz. pkgs. of cheese tortellini, cooked and drained
2 bunches of spinach, cleaned, cooked and chopped

Grease a 2-quart casserole dish; set aside. In a saucepan, over medium heat, combine butter and flour to create a thick paste. Pour in milk and stir until mixture is thick and bubbling. Add Parmesan cheese and blend until melted; stir in tortellini and spinach. Pour into prepared casserole dish and bake at 350 degrees for 30 minutes.

"Since 1984, Gooseberry Patch has been based around family, tradition, friendships and warmth. While our business continues to grow, we'll never be too big to forget about the two things that are most important to us...family and friends."

Jo Ann
1993

Lasagna Rolls

Kelli Keeton
Gooseberry Patch

When I was little, I remember standing on a chair next to my mom by the stove. I watched her roll these little bundles of noodles, meat and cheese and I would beg her to let me roll up a few. She always let me try some, and even though they were nothing compared to hers, she made me feel like they were perfect.

1 lb. mild or sage bulk sausage,
   browned and drained
8-oz. plus 3-oz. pkgs. cream
   cheese
1 bunch green onions, chopped

1 green pepper, diced
15-oz. jar spaghetti sauce
12 lasagna noodles, uncooked
1-1/2 c. mozzarella cheese,
   shredded

Combine sausage and cream cheese in the same skillet sausage was browned in. Cook over low heat until cream cheese melts. Stir in onion and green pepper; remove from heat. Spread half the spaghetti sauce in the bottom of a 13"x9" baking dish; set aside. Cook lasagna noodles according to package directions; remove from heat, leave in water. Lay one noodle flat on a cutting board and spoon one to 2 tablespoons of sausage mixture at one end of the noodle. Slowly roll the noodle and place in baking dish. Repeat with remaining noodles. Pour reserved sauce over top of rolls, top with mozzarella. Bake at 350 degrees for 15 to 20 minutes or until cheese has melted.

Dear Vickie & Jo Ann,

"I have only been a Gooseberry Patch customer for a few months, but I am a customer for life! I have enjoyed the Gooseberry books immensely! They have truly brought back little pleasures into my life and have helped me to enjoy my home, family and friends more."

Susan Wood, North Pitcher, NY

Shrimp Stuffed Chicken

Christi Miller
New Paris, PA

I like to make this when I'm planning an elegant dinner. I usually serve it with wild rice, dilled green beans and spinach salad.

4 lg. boneless chicken breasts
1/4 c. margarine
1/3 c. green onions, sliced
1 lb. mushrooms, sliced
3 T. all-purpose flour
salt and pepper to taste
3/4 c. chicken broth

1/3 c. dry white wine
1/2 c. milk
1 c. Swiss cheese, shredded, divided
1 lb. shrimp, shelled and deveined
1/3 c. bread crumbs

Pound the chicken breasts until 1/4-inch thick; set aside. Heat margarine in a large skillet over medium heat. Add onions and mushrooms; cook until tender. Sprinkle with flour, salt and pepper. Stir until well mixed. Add chicken broth, wine and milk. Simmer over medium heat until smooth. Add 1/2 cup of cheese and continue to cook until cheese melts; remove from heat. In a small bowl, combine shrimp and bread crumbs. Stir in 1/4 cup of sauce; mixing well. Divide into 8 equal portions. Place each portion in the center of chicken breast. Roll meat around stuffing and place seam side down in a lightly oiled baking dish. Pour remaining sauce over chicken. Bake at 375 degrees for 20 minutes. Sprinkle top with remaining cheese and bake 5 minutes longer. Serves 8.

Gooseberry Patch books and catalogs feature original illustrations produced by hand using pen and ink, colored pencils or watercolors.

Swedish Fish Bake

Leekay Bennett
Gooseberry Patch

Mom and Dad often entertained foreign guests. Once a visiting Scandinavian dignitary was so impressed with Seattle, and my mother's cooking, he immediately put a down payment on a house. Unfortunately, it was in Swedish Kronor and converted to only 98 cents in American money!

1 lb. white fish fillets
10-3/4 oz. can cream of celery
   soup
1 c. green beans, cooked

2 t. prepared horseradish
2 T. pimento, chopped
1/2 t. dried dill leaves, crushed

Arrange fish fillets in a 1-1/2 quart shallow baking dish. Bake at 350 degrees for 15 minutes; spoon off excess liquid. Combine remaining ingredients, pour over fish fillets. Bake 10 additional minutes or until fish is done. Remove fish to a platter; spoon sauce from baking dish over fillets before serving.

Robbie's "pulling up anchor" during a family fishing trip -1990

Gourmet Pot Roast

Grandpa Curly
Jo Ann's dad

This is a favorite recipe of mine...the Martin boys love it! The secret is to cook the roast very slowly so it comes out of the oven tender, then slice it very thin.

salt and pepper to taste
1/2 c. all-purpose flour
4 to 5 lb. beef pot roast
1-1/2 T. oil
2 onions, chopped
1/2 c. water
1/4 c. catsup
1/3 c. beef broth

1 clove garlic, minced
1/4 t. dry mustard
1/4 t. dried marjoram
1/4 t. dried rosemary
1/4 t. dried thyme
1 bay leaf
8-oz. can sliced mushrooms, undrained

Add salt and pepper to flour and coat roast well. Heat oil in a Dutch oven; add roast and brown on all sides. Add onions and continue to cook for 2 minutes. Stir in remaining ingredients, except mushrooms. Cover and bake at 300 degrees for 2-1/2 to 3 hours. Add mushrooms and their liquid, cover and cook an additional 30 minutes.

"Our families have supported us from the very beginning. I don't think Gooseberry Patch would be what it is today without the blessings of our families and all of the love and support Jo Ann and I have received from our husbands."

Vickie
1991

Penne Pasta with Tomatoes
Dana Stewart
Gooseberry Patch Artisan

I love this pasta dish in the winter when practically everything is out of season and I'm bored with all my "family standards."

6 T. olive oil
1-1/2 c. onion, chopped
1 t. garlic, minced
3 28-oz. cans Italian plum
   tomatoes, drained
2 t. basil
1-1/2 t. red pepper flakes
2 c. chicken broth

salt and pepper to taste
1 lb. penne pasta
2-1/2 c. havarti cheese, grated
1/2 c. Kalamata olives, sliced
1/2 c. fresh Parmesan cheese,
   grated
Garnish: 1/4 c. fresh basil,
   chopped

Heat 3 tablespoons oil in a Dutch oven over medium-high heat. Sauté onion and garlic 5 minutes. Add tomatoes, basil and red pepper flakes; bring to a boil. Break tomatoes with the back of a spoon, then add broth. Reduce heat and simmer one hour. Salt and pepper to taste; set aside. Cook pasta according to package direction; drain. Toss with remaining oil and combine with garlic sauce. Blend in cheese. Pour in a 13"x9" baking dish. Layer on olives then Parmesan. Bake 30 minutes at 375 degrees. Sprinkle fresh basil on top before serving. Serves 6 to 8.

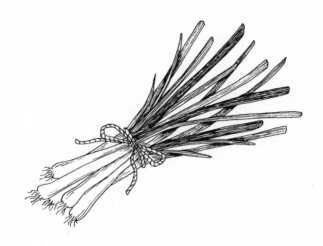

Two friends...still sharing stories across the backyard fence -1990

Matt & Emily cuddle up with Max -1987

Emily & Matt are all set for trick-or-treat! -1986

Jo Ann & Sydney share a smile for the camera -1999

Farmhouse Sides

Vickie, age 5, with Grandpa, Mom & Grandma, celebrating Grandpa's 85th birthday.

Herbed-Mushroom Potatoes
Susan Kennedy
Gooseberry Patch

A wonderful way to serve potatoes! It makes an elegant dinner served with a crown pork roast and sauerkraut!

1 T. extra virgin olive oil
1 T. garlic, minced
1/8 t. dried thyme, crumbled
1/8 t. salt
1/8 t. pepper
8-oz. can sm. white button
   mushrooms, quartered
4 oz. fresh shitake mushrooms,
   stems removed, caps halved
   and cut in strips

1/3 c. chicken broth
1-1/2 lbs. baking potatoes,
   peeled, chopped and cooked
3/4 c. buttermilk
1/2 t. salt
1/4 t. pepper
Garnish: 2 T. chives, chopped

Heat oil in a Dutch oven over medium heat. Stir in garlic, thyme, salt and pepper. Sauté until garlic is tender. Add mushrooms and cook one minute. Blend in chicken broth, bring to a boil then reduce heat and simmer 5 minutes. Remove from heat; cover. Mash with buttermilk; add salt and pepper. Spoon into a 2-quart serving dish. Layer mushrooms on top of potatoes; sprinkle with chives.

"When I was growing up, my mom had only one cook-book...but just about every favorite family recipe is in it! Time has taken its toll on many of the pages, but I still flip through it every once in awhile and think back to those days when I was a little girl in Mom's kitchen."

Vickie
1999

Zucchini Crescent Pie

Megan Bethel
Irwin, PA

Cut into wedges, this makes a wonderful side for your family's favorite pasta or seafood dish.

4 c. zucchini, thinly sliced
1 c. onion, chopped
1/2 c. margarine
1/2 c. parsley, chopped
1/2 t. salt
1/2 t. pepper

1/4 t. oregano
2 eggs, beaten
8 oz. mozzarella cheese, shredded
8-oz. tube crescent rolls

Preheat oven to 375 degrees. In skillet sauté zucchini and onion in margarine for 10 minutes. Stir in seasonings. Blend eggs and cheese and stir into vegetable mixture. Separate dough and place in an ungreased quiche pan; press together to form crust. Pour vegetable mixture on top of crust. Bake for 18 to 20 minutes. Let stand 10 minutes before cutting.

"Everyone laughs at this, but we were only able to pay my parents $2 an hour each when they first volunteered to help us. We were delighted they were part of the beginning of Gooseberry Patch."

Vickie
1996

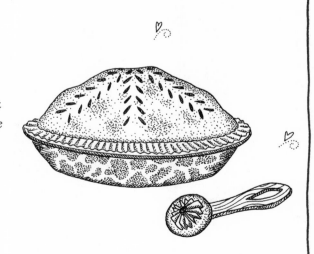

Summer Harvest

The Governor's Inn
Ludlow, VT

Here's the answer to what to do with all the zucchini and summer squash you plant in your garden each summer! This recipe easily reheats and makes a wonderful side dish.

2 onions, chopped
1-1/2 lbs. summer squash, chopped
1-1/2 lbs. zucchini, chopped
4 carrots, grated

2 c. sour cream
4 T. chicken bouillon
12-oz. pkg. cornbread stuffing
2 sticks sweet unsalted butter, melted

Preheat oven to 350 degrees. Steam onions, squash and zucchini until crisp-tender. In a large bowl combine carrots, sour cream and bouillon; add steamed vegetables and pour into greased baking pan. Mix stuffing and melted butter. Cover vegetable mixture with cornbread stuffing mixture. Bake for 45 minutes.

Happy Valentine's Day Emily!
-1987

Sweet & Sour Cabbage

Wendy Paffenroth
Pine Island, NY

An old-fashioned side dish.

2 T. butter
1 med. onion, diced
2 to 3 red apples, cored and
    chopped
2 to 3 T. apple cider vinegar

2 T. brown sugar
salt and pepper to taste
1 sm. head of cabbage, finely
    chopped

In a large pot, melt butter. Add onions and continue to cook until tender. Add apples and stir to coat. Add vinegar, brown sugar and salt and pepper; mix well. Stir in cabbage and cook 10 to 12 minutes or until tender. Remove and pour into a casserole dish. Bake at 325 degrees for 15 minutes, stirring halfway through cooking time. Makes 8 servings.

Herb Seasoned Beans

Debbie Cummons-Parker
Lakeview, OH

A favorite at our house each summer when fresh
green beans are in season!

1/2 c. water
4 c. fresh green beans
1/4 c. butter, melted

1/2 c. seasoned bread crumbs
2 t. fresh parsley, chopped

Add water and beans to a Dutch oven; simmer until beans are crisp-tender, about 15 minutes. Drain and set aside. Combine butter with remaining ingredients, mix well with beans. Serves 5.

Au Gratin Potatoes

Sara Wisecup
Winona, MN

Creamy and cheesy! Using red potatoes adds
a new twist to a familiar favorite.

1 stick butter
1/2 c. all-purpose flour
2 c. milk
1 c. American cheese, shredded

1 c. Cheddar cheese, shredded
salt and pepper to taste
5 lbs. red potatoes, chopped and
   cooked

Melt butter in a medium saucepan. Combine flour and milk, add to
butter and cook over medium heat until mixture thickens. Stir in
cheeses; salt and pepper to taste. Add potatoes to a large mixing bowl,
pour cheese mixture over top; gently mix. Spoon into a 3-quart
casserole dish. Bake at 350 degrees for 40 to 50 minutes. Remove
from oven and let stand 10 minutes before serving.

Crunchy Cauliflower

Eleanor Bierley
Miamisburg, OH

Tangy and crisp!

4 c. cauliflower flowerets
1/2 c. mayonnaise
1 t. dry mustard
1 green onion, chopped

Garnish: 1/2 c. sharp Cheddar
   cheese, shredded and
   1/4 c. sunflower seeds

Place cauliflower in a saucepan, cover with water and cook until
crisp-tender. Drain and place in a serving bowl. Combine mayonnaise,
mustard and onion and spoon over cauliflower. Sprinkle with cheese
and sunflower seeds. Serves 6.

Italian Zucchini

Julie Miller
Gooseberry Patch

A great side dish from Mom. I like to serve it over pasta, too.

4 c. zucchini, diced
1 c. onions, diced
1 green pepper, chopped
1/4 c. vegetable oil
15-oz. jar pizza sauce

salt and pepper
1 T. sugar
1 T. oregano
Garnish: grated Parmesan
cheese

Sauté zucchini, onions and green peppers in vegetable oil until crisp-tender. In a saucepan, mix pizza sauce, salt, pepper, sugar and oregano. Cover and simmer until zucchini is just tender. Top with grated cheese and serve.

Dear Vickie & Jo Ann,

"Thank you for the wonderful and unexpected surprise that only true country friends can give. I was thrilled to open the mailbox and find my complimentary copy of your newest cookbook with my family memory in it! I plan to buy copies of the book for everyone in my family as a very special Christmas gift!"

Kim Carpenter, Lomont, CO

Twice Baked Potato Casserole

Emily
Vickie's daughter

My mom and I make this casserole for special family occasions.
It's easy and the dish always comes home empty!

6 lg. potatoes
1-1/4 t. salt
1/4 t. pepper
1/4 c. butter
1 c. Cheddar cheese, shredded
1 c. hot milk

3 green onions, finely chopped
1/2 c. sour cream
Garnish: Cheddar cheese,
    shredded and green onions,
    chopped

Scrub potatoes. Pierce skins and bake at 425 degrees for 60 minutes. Cut potatoes and scoop out pulp; mash. Add salt, pepper, butter, and cheese; beat well. Add hot milk and beat until fluffy and cheese is melted. Stir in green onions and sour cream; blend. Reduce oven temperature to 375 degrees. Spoon potatoes into an 11"x7" baking dish. Sprinkle with cheese and green onions; bake 15 minutes.

Baked Macaroni & Cheese

Loretta Nichols
Vickie's mom

This was a favorite Friday night dish when Vickie was little.

1 c. macaroni, cooked and
    drained
1 c. soft bread crumbs
1 t. onion, chopped
1 c. Cheddar cheese, grated

1-1/2 c. milk
2 eggs, beaten
1 T. butter
salt, pepper and paprika to taste

Combine all ingredients well. Spoon into a well oiled one-quart baking dish. Bake at 375 degrees for 45 minutes or until bubbly and golden.

Home Run Bean Bake

Helen Murray
Piketon, OH

*Baked beans are always a favorite side dish at our home. Great
served with brats or hamburgers...always a hit!*

1 lb. dry red kidney beans
1 lb. dry Great Northern beans
1 T. salt
1 lb. kielbasa, sliced
2 T. water
3 med. onions, chopped
2 10-oz. bags frozen lima
   beans, thawed

2 med. baking apples, peeled,
   cored and chopped
4 garlic cloves, chopped
3/4 c. molasses
3/4 c. tomato sauce
1/2 c. Dijon mustard

Rinse and sort beans. Place beans and salt in a large saucepan, cover
with water and bring to a boil. Boil 2 minutes, turn off heat and cover
pan; let sit one hour. In a heavy skillet, add kielbasa and water. Cook
over medium heat 10 minutes. Add onions and continue to cook until
kielbasa is browned, about 10 minutes. Remove from skillet and set
aside. Drain soaked beans, reserving cooking liquid. Place beans in a
6-quart casserole dish, add lima beans, apples and garlic. Stir in kielbasa mixture. Combine molasses, tomato sauce and mustard; stir well.
Pour evenly over bean mixture. Add just
enough reserved bean cooking liquid
to cover the beans. Cover casserole
dish and bake at 350 degrees for
1-1/2 hours. Reduce heat to 275 and
continue to bake for another 6 hours.
Add more liquid to beans to keep them
moist during baking. Serves 16 to 20.

*Batter up...Matt knocks a
home run out of the ball park!
-1990*

Aunt Tillie's Green Beans
Barbara Czachowski
Dallas, TX

*This recipe is one that has been a favorite in our family for years.
Even though most of my family doesn't care for vegetables,
they always ask for seconds of this dish!*

2 14-1/2 oz. cans French-style   1/4 t. pepper
   green beans   1/4 c. onion, finely chopped
2 T. plus 1 t. butter, divided   1 c. sour cream
2 T. all-purpose flour   1/4 lb. Swiss cheese, grated
1/2 t. salt   1 c. corn flake cereal, crushed
1 t. sugar

Drain beans; set aside. Melt 2 tablespoons butter over low heat; blend
in flour. Stir in salt, sugar, pepper and onion. Add sour cream; stir until
smooth. Remove from heat and fold in green beans. Spoon mixture
into a 1-1/2 quart greased casserole dish. Sprinkle cheese over top.
Layer cereal over cheese. Melt remaining butter and drizzle over cereal.
Bake at 350 degrees for 30 minutes. Serves 6.

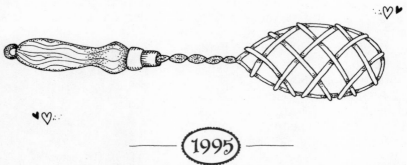

— (1995) —

Jo Ann & Vickie mailed a special edition of the "Goose Feathers"
newsletter to Gooseberry Patch customers in June 1995 asking
for recipes, memories and tips for three upcoming books. The
hundreds of responses they received became "Good For You!" and
"Homespun Christmas".

Stuffed Tomatoes

Ann-Marie Blentlinger
Chattanooga, TN

An old-fashioned recipe that goes well with special Sunday dinners.

4 to 6 med. tomatoes
garlic salt
2 10-oz. pkgs. chopped frozen
    spinach
1 sm. onion, minced
1 c. fresh Parmesan cheese,
    grated and divided

1/4 t. black pepper
1/4 t. cayenne pepper
1/2 c. Italian bread crumbs
2 eggs
6 T. butter, melted

Scoop pulp from tomatoes discard. Sprinkle tomatoes lightly with garlic salt and turn upside down on a paper towel to drain. Cook spinach according to package directions; drain and squeeze out water. Combine spinach with 1/2 cup Parmesan cheese and remaining ingredients; stuff tomatoes. Sprinkle tops with remaining cheese and bake at 350 degrees for 30 minutes.

*"I cooked at home a lot. My brothers
and sisters used to tease me
and call me 'Suzy Homemaker.'
They'd rather go outside to
play and I'd stay inside and
make brownies. My mother
would have dinner parties and I
loved to work in the kitchen and
help behind the scenes."*

**Jo Ann
1999**

Asparagus Casserole

Carol Sheets
Gooseberry Patch

This has been a family tradition for 2 generations. My husband's grandmother made this casserole for many holiday dinners, and it was expected to appear at all family gatherings. It is especially good made with fresh asparagus in the spring.

12 to 15 saltine crackers, crushed
1-1/2 lbs. fresh asparagus, chopped and cooked
10-3/4 oz. can cream of mushroom soup

1 c. milk
1/2 lb. sharp Cheddar cheese, grated
3 hard-boiled eggs, diced

Butter a 1-1/2 quart casserole and place ingredients in layers, starting and ending with crackers. Bake at 350 degrees for 30 minutes.

Diane, Teresa, Carol, and Becky (our customer satisfaction team) are the "cat's meow" at a Gooseberry Patch Halloween get-together! -1998

Peas & New Potatoes

Cheryl Bierley
Franklin, OH

*Fresh red potatoes are so tender, this favorite recipe
is ready in just a few minutes!*

1 slice bacon, diced
1 T. olive oil
1 c. red potatoes, diced

2 c. fresh peas
salt and pepper to taste

In a large skillet, combine bacon, olive oil and potato. Cook over
medium heat until bacon and potatoes begin to brown. Cover and
continue to cook 5 minutes or until potatoes are tender; stir in peas.
Cover and cook an additional 5 to 8 minutes or until peas are tender.
Season to taste. Serves 4.

Gingered Vegetables

Barbara Arnold
Toledo, OH

A crisp and tasty way to serve vegetables!

4 summer squash, sliced
1 red pepper, sliced
1 red onion, sliced
3/4 c. mushrooms, sliced

1/4 c. butter
3 Roma tomatoes, quartered
1 t. ginger

Sauté first 4 ingredients in butter until crisp-tender. Add tomatoes and
ginger. Simmer, covered, for 5 minutes. Serves 6.

Butternut Squash

Linda Dewhirst
Rock Port, MO

Use all the bounty in your harvest garden for this terrific side dish!

2 med. butternut squash
4 T. butter
4 T. brown sugar
4 t. balsamic vinegar
4 t. port or dry sherry
olive oil

2 carrots, cut into thin strips
2 zucchini, cut into thin strips
2 yellow squash, cut into thin
   strips
salt and pepper to taste

Preheat oven to 350 degrees. Slice butternut squash lengthwise and scoop out seeds. Use a paring knife to cut a diamond-shaped pattern in the fleshy part of the squash. Arrange squash in a baking dish and place one tablespoon each of butter and brown sugar in the hollow of each squash half. Sprinkle squash with balsamic vinegar and port wine or dry sherry. Cover with aluminum foil. Bake at 350 degrees for 1-1/2 to 2 hours. When squash is almost done, heat olive oil in a skillet and sauté the vegetables; salt and pepper to taste. Spoon vegetables over squash and serve.

"We absorbed all of our own expenses for the first three years. Any money we made we put right back into Gooseberry Patch. Then, in 1988, we started paying ourselves $100 a month. That's when we knew we were going to make it."

Jo Ann
1994

Fresh Creamed Corn

Susie Backus
Gooseberry Patch

This is a delicious way to use fresh corn from the garden.
When my sisters and I were young, we always called it
"corn on the cob, off the cob!"

6 ears corn
3/4 c. butter
1/2 c. light cream

1/2 t. sugar
salt and pepper to taste

Husk corn and slice kernels off with a sharp knife. Melt butter in a skillet, add corn and cook over medium-low heat 4 minutes. Add cream, sugar, salt and pepper; reduce heat to low. Cook 3 to 4 minutes, stirring continually.

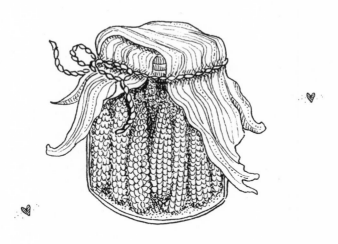

"We're always striving to keep Gooseberry Patch unique. We thought each step would get easier as we went along, but we've found we still face the same challenges as we did in 1984...they're just on a different level. It keeps things exciting. That's why we have to be a part of every detail!"

Jo Ann
1997

Squash Casserole

Paula Braswell
Marietta, GA

This recipe is my favorite! It was shared with me 30 years ago by my dear friend Diane. I have served it at many dinner parties and the men always love it, but are so surprised to find out it's squash!

2 c. squash, cooked and drained
1 stick margarine, melted
3 eggs, beaten
1 t. salt

1/2 t. pepper
1 c. onions, chopped
1 c. Cheddar cheese, grated
1 c. evaporated milk

Mash squash; add remaining ingredients and mix well. Pour into a greased 2-quart casserole. Bake at 375 degrees for 40 minutes or until casserole is firm in the center.

Sweet Onion Bake

Tracey Cate
Fremont, NE

Great as side dish or even spread over a thick, juicy hamburger!

2 med. sweet onions, sliced
10-3/4 oz. can cream of
  mushroom soup

1 c. Cheddar cheese, shredded
3/4 c. potato chips, crushed

Spray an 8"x8" baking dish with non-stick cooking spray. Place onions in pan, spread soup over top. Sprinkle with cheese and potato chips. Bake at 350 degrees for 30 to 40 minutes.

"The cookbooks were a natural spin-off to the catalog. They're fun for us, and for everyone who contributes to them."

Jo Ann
1998

Autumn Rice

Mark Demidovich
Charleston, SC

Served with grilled chicken and steamed vegetables, this is great!

1 med. onion, chopped
2 c. carrots, shredded
1/2 c. pecans, chopped
3/4 c. butter, divided
3 T. olive oil, divided
1 c. orzo
2 c. long grain wild rice

4 cloves garlic, minced
1 lb. mushrooms, sliced
1 c. fresh parsley, chopped
salt and pepper to taste
4-1/2 c. chicken broth
1 c. fresh Parmesan cheese, grated

In a large skillet, sauté onion, carrots and pecans in 1/4 cup butter and one tablespoon olive oil until brown; set aside in a large mixing bowl. In the same skillet, brown orzo and rice in 1/4 cup butter and one tablespoon olive oil; stir into onion mixture. Sauté garlic in remaining butter and olive oil, combine with mushrooms, parsley, salt and pepper; blend into rice mixture. Add broth, mixing well and spoon into a large saucepan. Simmer, covered, over low heat for 25 minutes. Transfer half of the rice mixture to a buttered 2-quart casserole dish; sprinkle with cheese. Top with remaining rice mixture and bake at 350 degrees for 25 minutes.

Happy Halloween! Emily smiles next to the Jack-o'-lantern Daddy helped her carve -1988

Nana's Carrot Ring

Lola Nason
Walnut Creek, CA

Over the years your catalog has given my husband and me many ideas. Recently, after 64 years of wonderful memories, my husband passed away. I'd like to share with you a recipe from his Scottish mother's family.

2 T. butter	3 egg yolks, beaten
2 T. all-purpose flour	3 egg whites, beaten
3/4 c. milk	1 c. carrots, chopped
1/2 c. Cheddar cheese, grated	1/8 t. nutmeg

Combine butter, flour, milk, cheese and egg yolks. Fold in egg whites, carrots and nutmeg. Place mixture in a lightly oiled ring mold. Bake one hour at 350 degrees. When done, place mold in water to help loosen carrot ring.

1987

Vickie & Jo Ann changed the style of the catalog in 1987 so it would feel more like a letter shared among country friends. In between catalogs, they also sent out a short, two-page flyer that felt very much like a letter from home.

Sweet CARROTS 5¢

source of Vitamin A

choice seeds GUARANTEED

Broccoli-Onion Deluxe

*Margaret Scoresby
Mount Vernon, OH*

A favorite for potlucks or church dinners.

10-oz. pkg. chopped frozen
   broccoli, thawed
2 c. sm. frozen whole onions
1/4 c. butter, divided
2 T. all-purpose flour
1/4 t. salt

1/8 t. pepper
1 c. milk
3-oz. pkg. cream cheese
1/2 c. grated Parmesan cheese
1 c. soft bread crumbs

Cook broccoli and onions as directed on package; drain. In saucepan, melt half of the butter. Blend in flour, salt and pepper; add milk. Cook, stirring constantly until thickened and bubbly. Blend in cream cheese until smooth. Place vegetables in a 1-1/2 quart casserole. Pour sauce over vegetables and mix lightly. Top with cheese. Melt the remaining butter, toss with bread crumbs and sprinkle on top of the casserole. Bake at 350 degrees 40 to 45 minutes or until heated through. Serves 6.

*"I remember my grandmother making me and my brothers and sisters
TV dinners when we used to stay at her house. My mother would
never, ever let us have them, but 'Nana' would sneak and fix them for
us on occasion. She'd let us set up TV trays in the living room and
we'd all sit together and watch whatever was on television that
night. I don't think mom ever knew."*

**Jo Ann
1998**

Block Party Beans

Betty McKay
Harmony, MN

A good recipe for large gatherings and potlucks. It's a always a favorite at our house.

2 c. onion, chopped
1 c. celery, chopped
2 lbs. ground beef, browned and
   drained
10-3/4 oz. can tomato soup
6-oz. can tomato paste
1/2 c. catsup
16-oz. can green beans, drained

17-oz. can lima beans, drained
15-1/2 oz. can butter beans,
   drained
15-1/2 oz. can kidney beans,
   drained
16-oz. can pork and beans
1/2 c. brown sugar, packed
2 T. mustard

Add onions and celery to browned ground beef, continue to cook until tender. Stir in soup, tomato paste and catsup, simmer 15 to 20 minutes. Spoon into a 3-quart casserole dish or roaster, add remaining ingredients; stir well. Bake uncovered at 350 degrees for one hour. Makes 25 servings.

Jo Ann & Sydney stop to enjoy an Independence Day bicycle parade and neighborhood party -1998

Garlic-Basil Mashed Potatoes   *Jo Ann*

Mashed potatoes are a very popular comfort food at Gooseberry Patch potlucks; we're always looking for new ways to serve them! Try this recipe, we think you'll like the garlic and basil combination.

10 cloves garlic, unpeeled
3 T. olive oil
9 med. potatoes, peeled and
    chopped
8 oz. sour cream
1/4 c. plus 3 T. grated Parmesan
    cheese, divided

1/4 t. salt
1/4 c. milk
1/4 c. fresh basil leaves,
    chopped

Place garlic in a soufflé dish. Drizzle olive oil over garlic and bake at 350 degrees for 20 minutes or until soft. Peel garlic, discarding skins and reserving oil. Add potatoes to a stockpot, cover with water and boil for 20 to 25 minutes or until tender; drain. Transfer potatoes to a large mixing bowl. Beat potatoes with an electric mixer on low speed. Add sour cream, 1/4 cup Parmesan cheese, baked garlic, reserved oil and salt. Gradually beat in enough milk until potatoes are fluffy; stir in basil. Spoon the potato mixture into a greased 2-quart casserole dish. Cover and bake at 325 degrees for 40 minutes. Stir; sprinkle with remaining Parmesan cheese. Bake, uncovered, 10 to 15 minutes or until heated through. Serves 10 to 12.

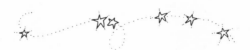

"I don't think our enthusiasm or energy has changed at all over time. This is still just as much fun today as it was when we first started."

Jo Ann
1995

Dilly Green Beans

Betty Stout
Worthington, OH

Best if you have fresh green beans right from the garden! We always have a large garden and plant different varieties of green beans to enjoy in this favorite recipe. It really brings the taste of summer back when you open a jar in the middle of winter.

2 heads fresh dill
2 hot peppers
2 cloves garlic, peeled
1/2 t. cayenne pepper

1 lb. fresh green beans
1-1/2 c. water
1 c. cider vinegar
2 T. salt

Divide dill, hot peppers, garlic and cayenne equally between two sterilized pint canning jars. Pack beans upright in each jar, dividing evenly. In a medium saucepan, bring water, vinegar and salt to a boil. Pour over beans, leaving 1/2 inch of head space. Add lids and screw rings down tightly. Process in a boiling water bath for 15 minutes. Makes 2 pints.

Dear Vickie & Jo Ann,

"I have been getting your country goodies for five years now. I love going out to my mailbox and having a special package from Gooseberry Patch waiting for me! Keep the wonderful surprises coming. You are country to a 'T'!"

Cindy Coughlin,
Binghamton, NY

Clam Fritters

Jan Walsh
Gooseberry Patch Artisan

My husband, Jack, and I harvest fresh shellfish from our beaches. On the occasions I don't make clam chowder, I mix up this batter and serve clam fritters with homemade tartar sauce.

1-1/2 c. all-purpose flour, sifted
2-1/4 t. baking powder
3/4 t. salt
2 egg yolks
3/4 c. milk

1-1/2 T. oil
1 egg white
20 clams, cleaned
oil

Sift flour, baking powder and salt together; set aside. In a medium bowl, beat egg yolks, milk and oil. Gradually add flour mixture, beating until smooth. Beat egg white until soft peaks form; fold into batter. Add enough oil to a deep fryer or heavy skillet to equal 2 to 3 inches. Dip clams into batter and deep fry a few at at time for 3 to 4 minutes. Clams will be golden in color and float to the surface when done. Drain on paper towels. Repeat with remaining clams.

"Vickie and I were once referred to in a magazine article as 'folksy little ladies.' I laugh about it, but we are just that. Although we run a successful business, we really are just country at heart."

Jo Ann
1995

Homemade Pink Applesauce

Joanne West
Beavercreek, OH

A family favorite that is always served with pork chops. The shade of pink will change depending on the color of the apple skins you use.

8 tart cooking apples, quartered
    and cored
1-1/2 c. cranberry juice cocktail

2 T. sugar
1 lemon, juiced

Combine all ingredients in a large saucepan. Over medium-high heat, bring to a boil; reduce heat. Simmer mixture until apples are soft, about 30 minutes. Remove from heat and cool slightly. Strain apples in a food mill; discard the skins. Refrigerate until ready to serve, or spoon into sterilized pint jars, seal and process in a boiling water bath for 15 minutes. Store sealed jars in a cool place.

Nectarine Slaw

Kathie Stout
Worthington, OH

Sweet and crisp...a nice change of pace!

1 c. plain yogurt
1 T. brown sugar
1 T. lemon juice

4 c. cabbage, shredded
1 lg. nectarine, sliced
1/2 c. peanuts, chopped

Combine first 3 ingredients; add cabbage. Refrigerate one hour. Add nectarine and peanuts before serving. Serves 6.

"Our cookbooks are our number one product and that's just great! Our customers are very involved...we couldn't do it without their help!"

Jo Ann
1998

Rice Pudding

Janice Carpentier
Aurora, IL

This old-fashioned side dish brings back memories of the love and laughter shared at my grandparents' house. Their home was always filled with the sights and smells of many old favorite Swedish dishes and my grandma gave me my love for cooking and baking. My grandparents have moved many miles away, but I am still very close to them. This delicious warm and creamy pudding was always one of my favorite dishes.

1/2 c. long cooking rice	1 t. vanilla extract
6 c. milk, divided	1 c. raisins
1/8 t. salt	1 t. lemon juice
3 eggs, beaten	Garnish: nutmeg
1/3 c. sugar	

Rinse rice well; set aside. Scald 4 cups milk, skim off foam; add rice. Add salt and cook over medium heat until mixture thickens. Add eggs, sugar, vanilla and remaining 2 cups milk. Stir in raisins and lemon juice; mix well. Transfer mixture to a greased 2-quart casserole dish; sprinkle with nutmeg. Bake at 325 degrees for one hour. Serves 8 to 10.

Vickie's mom & dad, Gooseberry Patch's first employees, at a Christmas party -1991

Croissant Stuffing

Kimm Auxier
Aurora, OR

I think this is the most delicious, tempting stuffing around!

1 lb. pork sausage
2 lg. onions, chopped
2 bunches of scallions, chopped
1 T. fresh thyme, chopped
1 T. fresh marjoram, chopped
1/2 t. fresh rosemary
12 day-old croissants, torn into
    bite-size pieces

2 c. plus 8 T. chicken broth,
    divided
salt and pepper to taste
1 c. all-purpose flour
2/3 c. champagne

Brown sausage, onions and scallions together in a medium frying pan. Add spices to the meat and onion mixture; stir well. Transfer mixture to a large mixing bowl, add torn pieces of croissants, 8 tablespoons broth, salt and pepper. Place stuffing in greased 2-1/2 quart casserole dish and bake at 350 degrees 15 to 20 minutes, or until warmed through. Combine flour, remaining broth and champagne together in a medium saucepan. Heat until mixture thickens; serve over stuffing.

"Gooseberry Patch has always represented home, family and tradition. That will never change. It's an important set of values that personally connects us to all of our customers."

Vickie
1991

Mashed Sweet Potatoes

Kimberly Grace
Sheffield Village, OH

This side dish was always requested by my father-in-law for Thanksgiving dinner. I can't make it without thinking about how he always complimented me on such a tasty dish.

5 to 6 med. sweet potatoes
20-oz. can of crushed pineapple, juice reserved

1/2 c. brown sugar, packed
1 t. ginger, finely minced

Peel and quarter sweet potatoes. Place in a large pot and cover with water. Boil 20 to 25 minutes or until tender. Drain well and mash. Add remaining of ingredients, reserving pineapple juice. Continue to mash sweet potatoes adding pineapple juice until potatoes are light and fluffy.

"We're incredibly selective when it comes to choosing items for the catalog. In fact, I'd say we're down-right picky. Of all the new products we see, probably one in every 100 makes it into the catalog."

Vickie
1998

New England Dressing

Nancy Molldrem
Eau Claire, WI

So good with turkey; it has a wonderful aroma and flavor.

5 lbs. potatoes
1/2 c. butter
1 lb. loaf day old bread
1-1/2 c. water
2 med. onions, finely chopped
1/4 c. green pepper, chopped

1/2 c. celery, chopped
2 t. salt
1/8 t. pepper
4 t. poultry seasoning
1/4 c. fresh parsley
1/2 t. paprika

Peel potatoes and cook in salted water until tender, about 20 minutes. Drain and mash with butter until fluffy; cool. Cut bread into 1/2-inch cubes and cover with water. Add onions, green pepper, celery, seasonings and parsley. Blend in potatoes and mix well. Pack lightly into a turkey and follow directions for roasting turkey, or spoon into a 2-quart casserole dish and bake at 350 degrees for 45 minutes.

"We love what we do. It's that simple. We love what Gooseberry Patch represents and we're proud of what we have to offer and how far we've come. We've built a company that we have a real fondness for and it's become a part of our lives."

Vickie
1999

Spinach-Potato Bake

Kris Lammers
Gooseberry Patch Artisan

This recipe was shared with me several years ago by a good friend. A great way to use leftover mashed potatoes...even the kids love it!

10-oz. box frozen chopped
   spinach
8 c. mashed potatoes, heated

1/2 c. sour cream
2 c. Cheddar cheese, shredded
2.8-oz. can French-fried onions

Thaw, drain and squeeze liquid from spinach. Stir together potatoes, spinach and sour cream. Spread in a lightly buttered 13"x9" dish; top with cheese. Bake at 350 degrees for 20 minutes, or until heated through. Remove from oven, sprinkle with French-fried onions, and return to oven for 10 minutes.

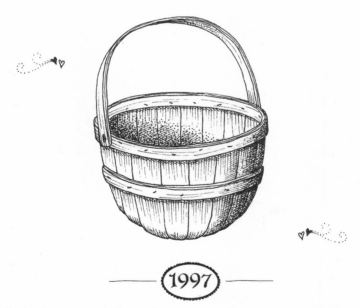

1997

Vickie & Jo Ann moved Gooseberry Patch from four different locations before moving into our very own building in the country in 1997. The move marked the first time the entire company was housed all under one roof.

Glazed Carrots

Bernadette Sanborn
Mt. Pacono, PA

This easy version of glazed carrots adds to any menu; it always seems to be a favorite in our family.

5 lbs. carrots, peeled and sliced
3 T. butter
1/4 c. light corn syrup

1/2 t. onion powder
salt and pepper to taste

Place carrots in a large saucepan; cover with water. Cook over medium heat until tender; drain. Add butter, corn syrup, onion powder, salt and pepper; stir to coat. Continue to cook over medium heat until carrots are glazed and heated through. Serves 8.

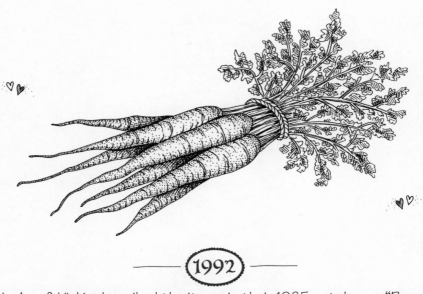

1992

Jo Ann & Vickie described the items in their 1985 catalog as "Proper Country Accessories." The phrase stuck and became the catalog banner until "A Country Store In Your Mailbox®" replaced it in the Spring of 1992.

Escalloped Corn

Susan Ingersoll
Gooseberry Patch Artisan

My grandmother is known by this simple, yet delicious recipe.
It's a family favorite at all dinners.

2 14-3/4 oz. cans cream-style
     corn
1 t. sugar
1 t. salt
2 eggs

1/4 t. pepper
1-1/2 c. milk
1 T. butter
1/2 c. soda crackers, crushed

Combine all ingredients together; blending well. Pour into a greased soufflé dish. Bake at 350 degrees for one hour, or until a knife inserted in the center comes out clean.

Dear Vickie & Jo Ann,

"Thanks so much for being inspired to start this wonderful business and for keeping it so friendly. The drawings in your books and catalogs are lovely and your telephone operators are very sweet!"

Margie Bertucci, Fort Wainwright, AK

Vickie's mom waves
"Goodbye" at her
retirement party -1994

Kaiser with Ryan,
Robbie & Kyle
-1996

Shelby, Matt & Vickie
at a backyard barbecue
-1997

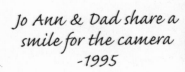

Jo Ann & Dad share a
smile for the camera
-1995

Sweet Celebrations

Vickie, age 2 celebrating her birthday at Grandma & Grandpa's house

CLARK FARMS Ice Cream

Lazy Daisy Cake

Jo Anne Muenzmaier
Brookfield, WI

This cake has such old-fashioned goodness and simplicity. I can picture Mom outside raking leaves, the scents of fall filling the cool, crisp air. We'd come home from school, greet Mom outside and step into the kitchen to be welcomed by the smell of warm brown sugar and coconut from this cake...delicious!

1 c. all-purpose flour	2 eggs, beaten
1 t. baking powder	1/2 c. milk
3/4 t. salt	1 t. butter
1 c. sugar	1 t. vanilla extract

Sift together flour, baking powder and salt; set aside. Gradually add sugar to eggs; beat until fluffy. Add flour mixture to egg mixture; beat thoroughly. Heat milk and butter to a boiling point. Add to the batter. Stir in vanilla and beat slightly. Pour into a greased 8"x8" pan. Bake at 350 degrees for 30 minutes. When done, spread immediately with topping and place under broiler until browned.

Topping:

5 T. brown sugar, packed	1/2 c. shredded coconut
3 T. cream	1/2 c. pecans, chopped
3 T. butter	

Mix all ingredients together and heat until topping is of a consistency to spread on top of the cake.

Grandpa's Peanut Butter Cookies

*Matt
Vickie's son*

I remember having fun with my grandpa...he always danced this funny little jig that made me laugh. Sometimes he'd let me dig potatoes in his garden and even ride on his tractor, but most of all, I remember the peanut butter cookies he made just for me...they were the best.

3/4 c. extra crunchy peanut butter
1/2 c. shortening
1-1/4 c. light brown sugar, packed
3 T. milk

1 T. vanilla extract
1 egg
1-3/4 c. all-purpose flour
3/4 t. salt
3/4 t. baking soda

Combine peanut butter, shortening, brown sugar, milk and vanilla. Beat with mixer on medium speed until well blended. Add egg and beat just until blended. Combine dry ingredients. Add to creamed mixture at low speed; blend. Drop by heaping teaspoonfuls onto an ungreased baking sheet. Flatten slightly in crisscross pattern with tines of a fork. Sprinkle on sugar, if you wish. Bake at 375 degrees for 7 to 8 minutes, or until set and just beginning to brown. Makes 3 dozen cookies.

*Grandpa & Matt;
super friends!
-1981*

Date Pudding

Beth & Chuck Reynolds
Gooseberry Patch Artisans

This recipe has been in our family for generations, and is always on the Thanksgiving and Christmas dinner tables.

1 t. baking soda
1 c. dates, chopped
1 T. butter
1 c. boiling water
1 egg

1 c. all-purpose flour
1 c. sugar
1/2 c. nuts, chopped
1/8 t. salt
16 oz. whipped topping

Combine baking soda, dates and butter; pour boiling water over top; don't stir. When mixture has cooled, add egg, flour, sugar, nuts and salt. Spread in a 13"x9" baking pan and bake at 350 degrees for 25 minutes. When cake has cooled, cut into bite-size cubes. Layer cake in a large glass bowl, alternating with layers of whipped topping.

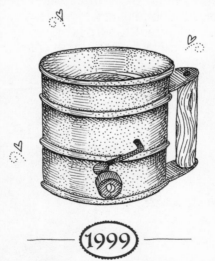

1999

Vickie & Jo Ann have provided a number of country artists with their first outlet for showing their crafts. Today, Gooseberry Patch works with more than 100 artisans who craft the nearly 400 items featured in the catalog.

Coffee Bars

Ruth Naples
Mexico, ME

This is a great old recipe I've made for years.

3 c. all-purpose flour
1 t. baking soda
1/2 t. salt
2 c. brown sugar, packed
2 eggs

1 c. warm coffee
1 c. oil
1 t. vanilla extract
1/2 c. chocolate chips
1/2 c. nuts, chopped

Sift together flour, soda and salt. Stir in brown sugar. In a separate bowl, combine eggs, coffee, oil and vanilla. Mix with dry ingredients. Spread mixture into greased 15"x10" baking pan. Sprinkle evenly with chocolate chips and nuts. Bake at 350 degrees for 25 to 30 minutes.

"We don't want to get caught up in the world of high-tech companies that are out there today. It's the personal touch we care about. We just want to have fun and continue to keep the friendships we've made with our customers."

Vickie
1995

Grandma's Butterscotch Pie

Sandra Curtis
Centerville, OH

Just the thought of this cake makes my mouth water! It brings back such memories of watching Grandma make it!

1 c. dark brown sugar, packed
4 T. all-purpose flour
1-1/2 c. whole milk
2 T. butter

2 eggs, separated
2 T. sugar
9-inch pie crust, baked

Mix brown sugar and flour together in a saucepan. Stir in milk and bring to a boil. Stirring constantly, add butter and egg yolks. Return mixture to a boil and pour into pie crust. Beat reserved egg whites until foamy then beat in sugar until stiff peaks form. Spread meringue on top of pie. Bake at 350 degrees until brown. Chill until ready to serve.

Matt gets a warm hug from Grandma following his high school graduation ceremony -1997

Velvet Shortbread Cutouts

Nancy Kirkelie
Lebanon, OR

I could never find a light and soft sugar cookie recipe that
I liked until I found this one...it's wonderful!

2 c. butter, softened
8-oz. pkg. cream cheese,
   softened
2 c. sugar

2 egg yolks
1 t. vanilla extract
4-1/2 c. all-purpose flour

Cream together butter and cream cheese until fluffy. Add sugar, egg yolks and vanilla; blend in flour. Cover and chill 2 hours Roll out to 1/4 inch thick; cut with cookie cutters. Bake at 350 degrees on a lightly oiled baking sheet 10 to 12 minutes. Cool on a wire rack.

Chocolate Crinkles

Patricia Smith
St. Johns, MI

A favorite for chocolate lovers!

3 eggs, beaten
1-1/2 c. sugar
4 4-oz. squares unsweetened
   chocolate, melted
1/2 c. oil

2 t. baking powder
2 t. vanilla extract
2 c. all-purpose flour
powdered sugar

Beat first 6 ingredients together; blend in flour. Refrigerate for one to 2 hours or until dough is firm. Using teaspoon-size balls of dough, roll in powdered sugar. Place 2 inches apart on ungreased cookie sheet. Bake at 375 degrees for 10 to 12 minutes.

Missouri Brownies

Nancy & Mike Marion
Gooseberry Patch Artisans

Very few church dinners or community functions were without Grandma Beth's Missouri Brownies...and if she tried another concoction, there was disappointment among the crowd.

2 c. all-purpose flour
2 c. sugar
4 T. cocoa
1 c. cold water
1 stick margarine

1/2 c. oil
1/2 c. buttermilk
1 t. baking soda
2 eggs

Sift dry ingredients together; set aside. Combine water, margarine and oil; bring to a boil. Pour over dry ingredients and beat until creamy. Add buttermilk, baking soda and eggs; mix well. Pour in a greased and floured jelly roll pan. Bake at 400 degrees for 18 minutes.

Frosting:

1/2 c. margarine
1/4 c. cocoa
1/3 c. buttermilk

16-oz. box powdered sugar
1/2 t. vanilla extract
1/4 to 1/2 c. nuts, chopped

Combine margarine, cocoa and buttermilk in a saucepan; bring to a boil. Add powdered sugar and vanilla; beat until smooth. Add nuts to taste and spread over warm brownies.

"We're always on the lookout for ideas when we go to flea markets together...not just for our homes, but for new products, too. We keep thinking ahead to the next catalog or the next book. We get so excited, we just can't help it!"

Vickie
1999

Sweet Celebrations

Soft Southern Sugar Cookies
Liz Kenneweg
Gooseberry Patch

This recipe is from a very old cookbook that belonged to my mother.

3/4 c. butter
1-1/2 c. sugar
2 eggs
2-1/2 c. all-purpose flour
2 t. baking powder

1/2 t. salt
1/2 c. milk
1 t. vanilla extract
7 oz. semi-sweet chocolate bar, chopped

Cream butter and sugar thoroughly. Add eggs, one at a time, and beat well after each addition. Sift together flour, baking powder and salt. Add to sugar mixture alternately with milk. Blend in vanilla and chocolate. Pour into a greased 15"x9" pan. Bake at 350 degrees for 30 minutes. Makes 4 dozen cookies.

"Customers send us pictures of their families all the time; it's fun to watch their children grow up and see pictures of family vacations. We have a special bulletin board for all the photos and letters we receive so everyone at Gooseberry Patch can read and enjoy them."

Jo Ann
1999

Gooseberry Crème Pie

Ruby Robert
Severy, KS

When I was young, my mother and I would go to the pasture and pick gooseberries, blackberries and any other kind of berry that we could make cobblers, pies or jellies with. There was nothing better than coming home from school and smelling freshly baked bread, topped with butter Mother had churned and elderberry jelly she had made.

1 T. butter	2-1/2 T. cornstarch
1 c. plus 1/4 c. sugar	1/4 t. salt
2 c. gooseberries	1/4 c. cream
3 egg yolks, beaten	9-inch pie crust, baked

In a saucepan, combine butter, one cup sugar and gooseberries. Cook over low heat, stirring continuously, until a liquid forms. Continue to cook until berries pop: remove saucepan from heat. Mix together egg yolks, remaining sugar, cornstarch, salt and cream. Add to gooseberry mixture, return to heat and boil until mixture is thick. Pour into pie crust and top with meringue.

Meringue:

4 egg whites	1/8 t. cream of tartar
1 t. vanilla extract	1 c. powdered sugar, sifted

Beat egg whites until foamy. Add vanilla and cream of tartar; stir. Add one teaspoon of powdered sugar at a time while continuously beating egg white mixture until stiff peaks form. Spread over pie filling and brown lightly in a 325 degree oven for 10 minutes or until lightly browned. Serves 6.

Sweet Celebrations

Family Favorite Crumb Cake
Jo Ann

A great take-along for the kids during soccer games!

1-1/4 c. all-purpose flour
2/3 c. brown sugar, packed
3/4 t. cinnamon
1/8 t. salt
1/4 c. butter

1/2 t. baking powder
1/2 t. baking soda
1/2 c. buttermilk
1 t. vanilla extract
1 lg. egg

Combine flour, brown sugar, cinnamon and salt in a bowl; cut in butter until mixture resembles coarse meal. Reserve 1/2 cup for topping; set aside. Add baking powder and baking soda to flour mixture; blend in buttermilk, vanilla and egg. Using a mixer, beat at medium speed until well blended. Coat an 8" round cake pan with cooking spray, spoon batter into pan. Sprinkle reserved topping over batter. Bake at 350 degrees for 30 minutes. Cool on a wire rack. Serves 8.

Martin Family Photo
Sydney, Jo Ann, Jay, Ryan, Kyle & Robbie -1997

Fresh Berry Pie

Mary Murray
Gooseberry Patch

I like to make this with any fresh fruit...mulberries
or red raspberries are just as good!

2 c. plus 1/4 c. all-purpose flour, divided
1 t. salt
2/3 c. butter, chilled
1/4 c. ice water

1 c. plus 1 T. sugar, divided
5-1/4 c. fresh blackberries
2 T. lemon juice
1 T. milk
Garnish: whipped topping

Combine 2 cups flour and salt in a large bowl. Cut in butter until mixture resembles coarse meal. Gradually blend in enough water to bind dry ingredients together. Divide dough in half and flatten each half; wrap in plastic and refrigerate one hour. Combine one cup sugar with 1/4 cup flour; add berries and lemon juice; toss. Roll out one half of dough on a lightly floured surface to a 12-inch round; transfer to a pie pan. Spoon filling into crust. Roll remaining half of dough into a 12-inch round, place over filling. Press edges together to seal then crimp edges. Cut slits in the top crust to vent steam. Brush milk over top crust, sprinkle with remaining sugar. Bake at 350 degrees for 45 minutes or until crust is golden. Serve with whipped topping.

Dear Vickie & Jo Ann,

"Thank you for such an amazing catalog! It feels like a nice big piece of apple pie on a beautiful fall day!"

Lisa DiNardo,
Lynchburg, VA

Peach Praline Cake

Barbara Lohmeier
Silver Spring, MD

Using fresh peaches makes this cake outstanding!
It has such a wonderful flavor!

16 oz. angel food cake
1/2 c. butter, softened
1/2 c. brown sugar, packed
1 c. powdered sugar
3 egg yolks
2 T. peach extract

6 med. fresh peaches, peeled
  and chopped
16 oz. whipped topping
12-oz. bag toffee chips
Garnish: peach slices

Cut angel food cake in half horizontally; set aside. Cream butter and sugars; beat until fluffy. Add egg yolks, beating well after each addition and stir in extract. Spread butter mixture on bottom layer of cake, layer on peaches, add top layer of cake. Combine whipped topping with toffee bits, folding gently. Spread mixture on cake. Cover cake and refrigerate for 4 hours or overnight. Garnish with additional peach slices.

"Our Gooseberry Patch customers are like family. Writing the cookbooks has only helped to make that relationship even stronger. It's a way for all of us to share and keep in touch with each other."

Vickie
1994

207

Grandma's Pudding

Veda Hutchins
Vickie's mother-in-law

This is a recipe I've made for three generations of kids...grandkids, great grandkids and now great-great grandkids!

1/4 c. creamy peanut butter
2 c. milk, divided
3-1/2 oz. box chocolate pudding
1/2 t. maple extract

Garnish: whipped cream, sprinkles, cherries or strawberries

Whisk peanut butter into one cup milk. Add remaining milk and slowly add dry pudding, whisking constantly. Add maple extract and continue to whisk until pudding thickens. Pour into individual custard cups. Refrigerate. Garnish with whipped cream, sprinkles and a cherry or strawberry on top. Makes 5 small servings.

Merry Christmas! Grandma Veda admires her new muffin basket from Gooseberry Patch -1998

Sweet Celebrations

Sea Foam
Vickie

This was one of my dad's favorite candy recipes.

2 c. sugar
1/2 c. water
1/8 t. salt

1/8 t. cream of tartar
2 egg whites, stiffly beaten
1 t. vanilla extract

Combine sugar, water, salt and cream of tartar. Cover and boil 5 minutes; uncover. Boil, without stirring, until mixture reaches the firm ball stage, 245 to 248 degrees. Pour slowly, beating constantly, into egg whites. Continue to beat until candy holds its shape. Add vanilla. Drop by teaspoonfuls onto wax paper. Let cool.

Strawberry Trifle
Beth & Chuck Reynolds
Gooseberry Patch Artisans

The number one dessert choice in our home!

2 8-oz. pkgs. cream cheese
2 c. powdered sugar
1 c. sour cream
1-1/2 t. vanilla extract, divided
1/4 t. almond extract

1/2 pt. whipping cream
4 T. sugar, divided
1 angel food cake, cubed
2 qts. strawberries, sliced

Cream together cream cheese and powdered sugar. Add sour cream, 1/2 teaspoon vanilla extract and almond extract; set aside. Blend whipping cream, remaining vanilla and one tablespoon sugar, fold into cream cheese mixture. Add angel food cake pieces. Combine strawberries and remaining sugar. In a large glass bowl, layer strawberries then cake mixture. Continue layering, ending with strawberries as top.

209

Chocolate Fudge

Vickie

One of my fondest memories is of Mother and me making fudge on Saturday nights. I still have the old recipe book with the original recipe in it. Sometimes we rushed it a bit and it wouldn't come out right, so we'd laugh and eat it spooned over ice cream instead!

2 c. sugar
2/3 c. milk
2 T. butter

6 T. cocoa
1 T. vanilla extract

Combine sugar, milk, butter and cocoa; bring to a boil. Continue to boil until mixture reaches the soft ball stage, 234 to 238 degrees. Add vanilla and cool. Beat until mixture is creamy and thick. Pour into a well buttered 13"x9" pan. Cut in squares.

Old-Fashioned Caramels

Vickie

So buttery and rich, a holiday favorite growing up. We wrapped ours in wax paper.

2 c. sugar
2 c. cream

1-3/4 c. corn syrup
1 c. butter

Combine sugar, one cup cream, corn syrup and butter; boil 30 minutes. Add remaining cream and boil to firm ball stage, 248 degrees on a candy thermometer. Pour into a well buttered 13"x9" pan. Cool completely and cut into squares.

Jo Ann & Vickie received their first national award in 1993 for the Harvest '92 catalog. Gooseberry Patch won a silver medal in the and was named one of the country's best catalogs.

Pineapple Tarts

Katherine Meredith
Greeneville, TN

This was the first dish I ever prepared for my husband…it became our breakfast, lunch and dinner! I can still see our first apartment and the beautiful stoneware platter piled high with tarts sitting on our dining room table, I thought they were a work of art!

3-oz. pkg. cream cheese
1/4 lb. butter
1 c. all-purpose flour

1/4 t. salt
8-oz. jar pineapple preserves

Mix all ingredients together except preserves. Roll into 2-inch balls. Refrigerate for 3 hours or overnight. Roll into flat circles on floured board or pastry cloth. Put scant teaspoon of pineapple preserves on pastry. Fold over to close and press edges with fork to seal. Bake on ungreased cookie sheet at 350 degrees for 15 to 20 minutes or until lightly browned. Cool on wire racks.

♥♡

"Vickie and I still get together every week to sit down over a cup of coffee and just chat. We talk about the kids, our husbands and when the next flea market or craft show is coming to town!"

Jo Ann
1991

Nana's Ricotta Pie

Regina Ferrigno
Gooseberry Patch

This pie is a special treat...our family always starts out the
Christmas holiday by enjoying a slice for breakfast!

1 lb. ricotta cheese, mashed
1/2 c. sugar
1 t. cinnamon
5 eggs, beaten

1/2 c. milk
1 lemon, juiced
1/2 sm. jar citron
10-inch pie crust, baked

Combine ricotta cheese, sugar and cinnamon together. Mix well and
add beaten eggs. Blend together, add milk and lemon juice. Fold in
citron. Pour into prepared pie crust and bake at 400 degrees for 10
minutes then reduce heat to 350 degrees and continue to bake until
light brown, about 40 minutes. Pie is done when it puffs up and
cracks. Knife should be clean when inserted about one inch from edge.

Brown Sugar Cookies

Lisa Watkins
Gooseberry Patch

A hint of maple flavoring makes these cookies special!

2-1/3 c. brown sugar, packed
1 c. butter, softened
2 eggs

1 t. vanilla extract
1/2 t. maple extract
2 c. all-purpose flour

Combine first 5 ingredients; blend well. Stir in flour until well blended.
Drop dough by teaspoonfuls on an ungreased cookie sheet. Bake at
375 degrees for 8 minutes. Makes 3 dozen cookies.

Friendship Delight

Lisa Engelhardt
Tavernier, FL

My husband and I moved to a new town right after we were married. I didn't know anyone and I was beginning my first teaching job. Melinda was one of the first friends I made at my new school and from day one, she shared many of her delicious recipes with me. It was a great ice breaker and made me feel as if I had another family. Now 13 years later we are still family and continue to share recipes.

1 c. all-purpose flour
1 c. pecans, chopped
1/2 c. butter, melted
1 c. powdered sugar
12 oz. whipped topping, divided
8-oz. pkg. cream cheese

4 c. milk, divided
4-oz. pkg. vanilla instant pudding
4-oz. pkg. chocolate instant pudding
nuts, chopped

Combine first 3 ingredients together and place in a 13"x9" pan. Bake at 325 degrees for 25 minutes or until lightly brown. Mix together powdered sugar and half the whipped topping. Blend in cream cheese. Spread over cooled crust. Mix 2 cups of milk with each pudding mix. Layer chocolate pudding over cream cheese layer, spread to edges. Layer vanilla pudding over chocolate pudding and top with remaining whipped topping. Sprinkle with nuts. Refrigerate 3 to 4 hours. Serves 10 to 12.

Across the backyard fence...Vickie & Jo Ann -1988

Peanut Butter & Fudge Pie

Coli Harrington
Gooseberry Patch

A yummy dessert! Peanut butter and chocolate
are such a terrific combination!

1/2 c. creamy peanut butter
1/4 c. honey
1 qt. vanilla ice cream, divided
6 oz. graham cracker pie crust

1/2 c. cashews, chopped,
   divided
6-oz. jar fudge topping
Garnish: whipped topping

Combine peanut butter and honey; blend in ice cream. Spoon half into the pie crust; sprinkle with half the cashews. Drizzle half the fudge topping over cashews; spoon remaining ice cream mixture over top. Sprinkle with remaining cashews and drizzle with fudge topping. Freeze until firm, about 6 hours. Garnish with whipped topping if desired.

Pumpkin Ice Cream

Carol Bull
Delaware, OH

A friend and I enjoyed this after a day of antiquing...it's wonderful!

1/3 c. brown sugar, packed
3/4 t. cinnamon

1 c. cooked pumpkin
4 c. vanilla ice cream, softened

In a large bowl, combine brown sugar, cinnamon and pumpkin; blend well. Fold in ice cream until thoroughly mixed. Spoon into a 9"x5" loaf pan; cover and freeze until solid.

Sweet Celebrations

Molasses Cookies

Laurie Williams
Gooseberry Patch Artisan

People claim that these cookies taste better if you chill the dough before you bake them...personally, I've never been able to wait that long! Grandma always kept a slice of bread in a cottage-shaped cookie jar, to keep the cookies soft; if there were any left to soften! She always had cookies on hand...and a hug.

1 c. butter
1 c. sugar
1 c. molasses

4 T. milk
4-1/2 c. all-purpose flour
2 t. baking soda

Cream together butter and sugar; add molasses and milk. Combine flour and baking soda; add slowly to the molasses mixture. Roll the dough into 2 logs, about the size of a paper towel tube. Slice the dough into 1/4-inch slices. Arrange on a greased cookie sheet. Bake at 350 degrees for 10 minutes.

Dear Vickie & Jo Ann,

"Thank you so much for the inspiration I received from your cookbook! You gave wonderful advice: 'Share a gift of cookies and bring a smile to someone's heart.' I volunteered to organize a Christmas cookie sale to help our church youth group raise money. We sold over 6,000 cookies and could have sold many more!"

Becky Stattelman
Ortonville, MN

Carrot Cake

Mavis Diment
Marcus, IA

*I remember taking this to my first family reunion and it was a big hit.
Several relatives asked for the "receipt" as Grandma called it.*

2 c. all-purpose flour
1 t. cinnamon
1 t. salt
2 t. baking soda
3 eggs, beaten
2 c. sugar
1 c. oil

2 c. carrots, shredded
8-oz. can crushed pineapple,
   undrained
1 c. walnuts
1 c. shredded coconut
1 c. raisins

Mix in order given and pour into greased 13"x9" cake pan. Bake at
350 degrees for 35 to 40 minutes or until done.

Silky Frosting:

8-oz. pkg. cream cheese,
   softened
1/2 c. butter, softened

1 T. lemon juice
1 t. lemon zest
1-1/2 c. powdered sugar

Cream first 4 ingredients together, then add powdered sugar. Mix well
and frost on cooled cake.

*Emily, Shelby & Matt
throw a birthday party
for Max...complete
with cake and party
hats! -1986*

Sweet Celebrations

Caramel Apple Cookie Pizza

Mel Wolk
St. Peters, MO

A great family treat that's so easy to prepare.

2 lg. apples, sliced
lemon juice
1 tube refrigerated sugar cookie
   dough
8-oz. pkg. cream cheese,
   softened

1/4 to 1/2 c. creamy peanut
   butter
6-oz. jar caramel ice cream
   topping
1/4 c. nuts, chopped

Soak apple slices in lemon juice to prevent browning; set aside. Press cookie dough into a 12" pizza pan. Bake according to package instructions. Remove from oven and cool. Combine cream cheese and peanut butter, spread over cooled crust. Arrange apple slices on top. Drizzle with caramel topping and sprinkle with nuts.

Rhubarb Crunch

Jeannine Aeikens
Sycamore, IL

Tart and crunchy...yummy!

1 c. all-purpose flour
3/4 c. quick-cooking oats
1 c. brown sugar, packed
1/2 c. butter, melted

1 c. sugar
1 c. water
1 T. cornstarch
4 c. rhubarb, chopped

Combine flour, oats, brown sugar and butter. Mix well and press half the mixture in an oiled 13"x9" baking pan. Combine sugar, water and cornstarch; bring to a boil. Continue to boil until clear; set aside. Place rhubarb on top of crust, pour hot cornstarch mixture over top. Sprinkle on reserved oat mixture. Bake at 350 degrees for one hour.

Oatmeal Cake

Tracy Onoz
Gooseberry Patch Artisan

Every year my mom bakes me the birthday cake of my choice, and this cake has been my request for the last several years.

1 c. long-cooking oats
1-1/4 c. boiling water
1 c. sugar
1 stick margarine
2 eggs, beaten
1-1/3 c. all-purpose flour
1 t. baking soda
1 t. cinnamon

1/2 t. salt
1/2 t. vanilla extract
1-1/2 c. brown sugar, packed
    and divided
1/4 c. evaporated milk
2 T. butter
7-oz. pkg. shredded coconut
1/2 c. walnuts, chopped

Combine oats and boiling water together; let stand 20 minutes. Combine next 8 ingredients. Blend in one cup brown sugar; add oatmeal. Pour mixture into a 13"x9" greased and floured pan. Bake at 375 degrees for 30 to 40 minutes. Combine remaining brown sugar, evaporated milk, butter, coconut and walnuts; spread on baked cake. Return to oven and brown topping under broiler.

Happy 5th Birthday Ryan!
-1988

Sydney wraps up in a new
coat from Grandma Tootsie
-1998

Matt & Emily
clowning around!
-Christmas 1997

Happy 1st Birthday Sydney!
Love, Robbie, Kyle & Ryan -1996

Emily & Sport smile for
the camera -1993

Index

Index

Index

We've cooked up a whole collection of Gooseberry Patch® books!

Have a taste for more? Call us toll-free at
1-800-854-6673

We'll send you our latest catalog filled with snowmen, Santas, ornaments, candles, cookie cutters, gourmet goodies, salt-glazed pottery collectibles and MORE...including our best-selling cookbooks!

Phone us:
1·800·854·6673

Fax us:
1·740·363·7225

Visit our website:
www.gooseberrypatch.com

Send us your favorite recipe!

*and the memory that makes it special for you!** We're putting together a brand new **Gooseberry Patch** cookbook, and you're invited to participate. If we select your recipe, your name will appear right along with it...and you'll receive a FREE copy of the book! Mail to:

Vickie & Jo Ann
Gooseberry Patch, Dept. BOOK
P.O. Box 190
Delaware, Ohio 43015

*Please help us by including the number of servings and all other necessary information!

Grandma traditions holidays memories

comfort food homemade pie simple pleasures home sweet home laughter

caring love

reunions

picnics

pictures

children

favorite recipes

family friends kitchen together smiles